14 to 41

**Freedom From Addictions
By Walking Through Life With Jesus**

By Shane Tempel

Unless otherwise indicated, all scripture quotations are taken from the King James Version of the Bible in the public domain.

Copyright © 2022 Shane Tempel
All rights reserved.

Cover photo by: Heart of Wyoming Photography
Author photo by: Wright Photography

14to41
Freedom From Addictions
By Walking Through Life With Jesus

ISBN: 979-8-9860400-2-8

	Dedication..6	
Chapter 1	On the Wrong Path............................7	
Chapter 2	Open Doors 12	
Chapter 3	Addictions...16	
Chapter 4	Summer Sadness...............................22	
Chapter 5	Compounding Addictions...................25	
Chapter 6	Demonic Visitors 29	
Chapter 7	Chemical Addictions.........................33	
Chapter 8	Young Love 39	
Chapter 9	Walking the Straight Line..................43	
Chapter 10	Crossing State Lines.........................47	
Chapter 11	The City Calls...................................53	
Chapter 12	Party On..57	
Chapter 13	Reality Check....................................62	
Chapter 14	Going Home......................................66	
Chapter 15	Moving On..71	
Chapter 16	The Wicked Woman 75	
Chapter 17	The Last Straw..................................79	
Chapter 18	A Second Chance..............................83	
Chapter 19	Dangerous Dreams............................87	
Chapter 20	My Exodus..92	
Chapter 21	Spiritual Visitors...............................96	
Chapter 22	The Enemy..100	
Chapter 23	Headed South....................................103	

Chapter 24	A Mistake	106
Chapter 25	The Bar	109
Chapter 26	West Virginia	113
Chapter 27	Returning to Florida	117
Chapter 28	The Trip Home	120
Chapter 29	A New Scene	125
Chapter 30	Our Trailer Home	129
Chapter 31	Next-Door Neighbors	133
Chapter 32	She Arrives	136
Chapter 33	New Beginnings	140
Chapter 34	Coming Into Focus	144
Chapter 35	Marriage	147
Chapter 36	Troubles	151
Chapter 37	Divorce	155
Chapter 38	My Best Friend	159
Chapter 39	Times of Music	163
Chapter 40	Old Friends and Music	166
Chapter 41	Workplace Dating	169
Chapter 42	Dogs and God	174
Chapter 43	Second Chances and Endings	178
Chapter 44	Dating	181
Chapter 45	Dreams and Visions	185
Chapter 46	Searching	189
Chapter 47	Denver	192
Chapter 48	Colorado Calling	196

Chapter 49	Distractions	200
Chapter 50	Pentecost	204
Chapter 51	Repairs and Restoration	207
Chapter 52	Loneliness of Heart and Waiting	211
Chapter 53	Television Ministries	214
Chapter 54	Being Set Free	218
Chapter 55	Stress and Reservations	222
Chapter 56	God's Direction	226
Chapter 57	Closing Doors	230
Chapter 58	Moving Day	233
Chapter 59	Traveling	235
Chapter 60	Almost There	240
Chapter 61	Where Home Would Be	243
Chapter 62	Irvin In Denver	246
Chapter 63	Local Move	249
Chapter 64	The Next Move	252
Chapter 65	Baptism	255
Chapter 66	A New Me	259
Chapter 67	The Holy Spirit	263
Chapter 68	Healing	267
Chapter 69	Speak Lord	270
Chapter 70	Kingdom Driven	273
	In Closing	278
	Contact The Author	279

Dedication

This book is dedicated to my personal savior, the Lord Jesus Christ. It was He who helped me to overcome the many addictions that I had which are detailed within this book. His grace and mercy cannot be measured and it is by walking with Him that I have victory every day and have been set free!

Chapter 1

On the Wrong Path

My story begins long ago as a struggling teenager trying to find his way. I just wanted to be me at the time, nothing more. I considered myself a normal kid; I tried out for sports and then later music, in particular marching band. I did not think in terms of geek, nerd, or jock until junior high and high school and that is when things changed. Sports was not my thing, I enjoyed watching the professionals on television like most kids but never did fully participate in sports in school. There were times when we would play baseball or football in the neighborhood but that was the extent of my playing days.

Looking back to my 8th grade year, that was the best time for friends and doing the things that adolescents do. There were some dark discoveries that year though, as I started smoking cigarettes and my best friend at the time exposed me to marijuana that would later become a gorilla on my back for years to come. Many things happened that year, including my horizons being opened to all kinds of music and my parents buying me my first guitar but it was the next year that would change the course of my life spiritually forever.

I had a paper route when I was younger and rode a red ten-speed bike, one day I was on one of the neighborhood streets, delivering papers and it happened. A bully accosted me. It started with one boy who was a grade or two above me. I was a freshman and was considered "new meat" by this particular person. Before I knew it there were two, then three bullies. They were like vultures circling their prey at times. It was mental torment and fearful situations for me day after day. It became so bad, that I quit my route but then had more encounters at school and on the bus, and throughout the neighborhood.

The really bad part about it was, one of the boys was in my grade but he was friends with the other two. These three bullies shall remain nameless because I will not give place to them or other bullies. The incredible hurt and harm that they have caused for so many victims of their cruel acts.

I was in a church at the time, although I was hardly living for God then, with smoking cigarettes and marijuana, drinking beer, and cussing regularly. However, at only fifteen years old I was in desperate need of someone to help me. My dad was an over-the-road truck driver and was hardly ever home. He was a good provider but that was a hard career for having a family life. My mother was a godly woman, who taught Sunday school, vacation Bible school, prayed over meals and took care of the house. She was a full-time stay-at-home mom but I did not think she could handle the bully situation or if she tried to address it by going to these boys' homes and talking to their parents, she would have only made things worse for me.

This was the mid-1980s in a small-town America where divorces were rare at the time and these boys had both moms and dads living at home. I was raised in the Methodist Church, which only had one service, once a week, on Sunday. At church I reached out to God the only way I knew how to, I would pray. I prayed and prayed and prayed but nothing happened that I could see or feel. I did not hear God; I don't believe I even felt God during that time. I was scared, living in fear, my dad or mom could not help me, my few friends were of no use in the situation, and in my cry for help, I felt God left me hanging out on a limb all by myself at the time.

I could never imagine the turn of events that was about to happen. I had a friend who one day came into the school cafeteria carrying a book. It was black and it was titled The Satanic Bible. Intrigued, I asked him what he was doing with it. He replied he was reading it for research. I found this very strange and perplexing at the time.

My friend was kind of a geek, being into technology and early gaming at the time, some would call him a nerd but he was my friend. I was desperate for answers and help with my situation, so I asked him if I could borrow it. A short time later he lent it to me and I began to read it. A whole new world opened up to me, literally. As I was reading this book, at the time and first glance, the book made sense to me on a secular, worldly level, to a fifteen-year-old boy.

It started plain enough, like treat others as they have treated you, almost the reverse of The Ten Commandments in The Holy Bible. I was intrigued, so I read on. Many things seemed to make sense; the book appealed to the flesh. The flesh is what I was dealing with and I did not know the spiritual things of life at that point in my young life. I do not recall how many chapters I read before I came to the chapter about putting curses on people and casting spells. It was a little way into the book.

As I write this, I plead the blood of Jesus over this topic, this thought process, and this writing. I ask for a complete shield of protection from the enemy as I put on the whole armor of God found in Ephesians 6:10-20.

I was in my second-story bedroom in the family home, one day after school and decided I was going to do this. I opened the book, read the enchantment or curse to put on the lead bully and as soon as I finished speaking, I felt a dark spirit whisk into my bedroom. It came right up beside me. Something happened that day; I opened a Pandora box and did not realize it until years later. Darkness had come into my life by my own tongue and words. The power of my own words had set me on a path of destruction and I did not even know it.

This all stemmed from a traumatic experience, bullying is a terrible thing that affects innumerable amounts of children each year and sadly many of them take their own lives as the only way out that they see. At the time that I was going through this, it was said boys will be boys and school principals would literally do nothing about it. Times have changed drastically with social media platforms and the twenty-four-hour-a-day news cycle that we live in. Whereas there is more information about bullying available but still sadly, many times nothing is done about it.

Well, I decided I was going to do something about it and I did. This was not the right thing to do but it is the path I chose. The next day after my encounter with the dark force in my room, I went to school and I felt different. I had confidence that I had not previously had in the midst of my situation. I had opened a door and stepped in, but I had no idea nor realized what I had done. This was a definite turning point that would take me down a dark winding road.

I continued to read The Satanic Bible but as I got further and deeper into the book it got darker and more evil with each turn of the page. I will not discuss anything further about the book but I will say, I stopped before I could finish it. What started, as a flesh-driven book for a carnal world was actually a work of pure evil. I gave the book back to my friend and was done with it. However, the damage had been done and had only just begun. There was a huge open door that I could not see through. I had to move forward but the enemy of my soul would not let me go, no, there would be many trials, battles, and tribulations to come.

Chapter 1 Takeaway: Overcoming Fear

Great fear had been introduced into my life at a young age. When faced with fear or fearful circumstance how do you overcome it?

Bible verses to reflect upon:
Proverbs 3:25-26
I John 4:18

_____
_____
_____
_____
_____
_____
_____
_____
_____
_____
_____
_____

Chapter 2

Open Doors

The other open door that had come into my life was music. I had started out listening to the Top 40 pop and light rock music of the late 1970s and 1980s as a child. I remember listening to the program of the same name with Casey Kasem. By the time I was tormented by bullies my taste in music had changed along with my marijuana usage.

As one might suspect, I got into the late 1960s psychedelic music movement. This included artists like Jimi Hendrix, The Doors, and Led Zeppelin. Then later on I found hard rock bands like ACDC and Judas Priest. I enjoyed the hard rock; faster style of that music and that led me to the genre of heavy metal, speed metal, and even death metal in my college years later on.

My point is this; music is an open door for the enemy and dark spirits or light spirits to enter into your house. There is spiritual attachment to all forms of music, you can usher in the presence of the Lord or on the other side of the aisle, a dark spirit. The pop culture music of the 1980s dealt mostly with women, falling in love, or sexual escapades. I was, as a single teenager who was being bullied, not interested in any of those subjects. I was instead listening to all the dark stuff. Then there are the accusations that would come against me in the next two years from my affiliations and my own actions.

I am sad to say that during the time of bullying I also became a bully. I know it seems hard to imagine but I felt I needed to lash out and take my frustrations out on another boy. So, I did, and I am ashamed of my behavior at the time and have put all this at the feet of Jesus and asked for forgiveness for my actions and have had to forgive the boys that bullied me back then.

As I write this and share my story there are many people that I had to forgive to move on and ask others to forgive me as well. All things are possible through the Lord Jesus Christ. Those were incredibly tough years for me being in high school. Later on, I used to hear people say that their best years were when they were in high school and that they would like to go back, I cannot imagine going back to that time at all. We cannot live in the past though and when I bullied that particular individual, it was like wrestling and pinning him to the ground. I don't like to think about it but it is part of the detrimental effects of bullying and I had to repent of my actions and ask for forgiveness.

It is not easy to recall the events of those years but I rely on the Lord to help me through this, to write everything that needs to be told. The bully situation got better as I seemingly turned my life towards the dark side. I was smoking cigarettes and marijuana, listening to heavy metal music, and had walked away from church and God. I still went to church as my parents made me since I lived at home and was a teenager but I was going to a dry and dying church at the time, spiritually speaking. I did not feel God there and the church was not walking in truth by the time I stopped going a few years later.

In my sophomore year, there was one particular event that stands out to this day. I was going to the lockers on the second floor and as I came around the corner, the hallway parted. It was full of students; the lockers were on the left and classes were on the right. The hallway was packed with students and just like that, everyone got out of my way. I know now that there were demons with me; I did not know it at the time. This was around my sixteenth birthday in the fall of that year. My few friends at the time in the hallway were amazed at what had happened, I thought it was cool but kind of just brushed it off at the time as no big deal.

I will not list all the bands that I was into but at the time one of the biggest influences for me was the heavy metal band Metallica.

On the day of the hallway incident, I was wearing my custom-made jean jacket with a large Metallica skeleton patch on the back, along with many other band name logos at the time. I continued on my dark road of heavy metal and it only progressed and got heavier and darker as the months and years went on.

The other driving force leading me down the heavy metal road at the time was my male hormones. Yes, those adolescent raging hormones, that for me was out of control. Even back then, in the late 1980s, the radio was saturated with love songs, if you want to call them that. There were songs about lust, one-night stands, cheating hearts, and the rest. As a young man, the last thing I wanted to hear was any of that. With no girlfriend, being a virgin (who desperately wanted to lose that) and I hated the top 40 music that I once loved. There were only a couple of radio-friendly artists that appealed to me during the time. The desire for harder and faster music was largely fueled by this particular cause.

So, into the darkness of heavy metal, I went. Looking back on this, some of these bands were very evil. The lyrics from one group bothered me as I listened to them on and off until finally one day, I would stop listening to them. They were not secretive about who they were serving but for a time I enjoyed their very hard, fast music. Somehow though, I knew it was straight out of hell. My sophomore year continued as did the music spiral, I was on.

As a young man, I was heavily influenced by the bands I was listening to and had aspirations to be like them. I had been given my first guitar at the age of fourteen by my parents and learned to play some music by ear. Fueled by hatred and anger I mimicked my favorite artists with my guitar playing. During the first few years, it was truly a hobby as I had dreams but was not a serious player. I used to be amazed by how some professional musicians could do substance abuse to the degree that they did and still function. I now know without a doubt that these people had spirits living in them and or around them at all times. Addiction is another area that I am all too familiar with and struggled greatly with for many years.

Chapter 2 Takeaway:
Do Not Hate but Forgive

I had been hurt and allowed that hurt to turn into hate. How do you keep this from happening in your own life?

Bible verses to reflect upon:
Psalms 37:8
Mark 11:25

Chapter 3

Addictions

The first time I can remember smoking a cigarette and drinking a beer, I was nine. I was at my cousin's house out in the country and we were in the barn. It was evening and there were several other children there with me. This was a family gathering, late summer as it was warm and nice out. I remember the event but I am sure I had no idea of how to smoke; however, drinking a beer was as easy as if it was a can of soda. Sadly, something else happened, my cousin got his hands on his father's adult magazines.

I do not recall the name of the publication but it was full of naked women. I had never seen such a thing and did not even know what to think. In one evening, I had been introduced to smoking, drinking, and pornography. The adults that were there on the property had no idea of what we were doing. They thought we were just playing in the yard and barn. Shortly after this happened, I remember feeling horrible about it and confessed it to my mother. That is what most children would do.

That event was perhaps the first open door to the enemy and worldly addictions for me. Nine years old, my friends. I was in a church at the time too and did not expect these events to unfold. That same year I encountered more pornography. There are two places that this happened; the first was at another relative's house. He had a large collection of Playboy magazines at the time. Sadly, he kept them in the living room by a recliner and anyone could have found them.

As a young pre-teen boy, I had a best friend who happened to live next door to me. This was around 1981 and my friend's family was Catholic but his dad had a subscription to another men's magazine called Penthouse. Now at the time, about the only thing more pornographic in nature was a magazine named Hustler. It wasn't too long before we had our hands on those magazines as well. Within the next two years, by 1983 my friend and I were watching adult cable channels at the time, as they had subscriptions to those as well. These were Christian people or so they professed. I am not here to cast stones but if you are a Christian and following Christ's example what are you doing with pornography?

This is not easy to write but I feel in the Spirit that the spirit of shame comes from these areas and that I need to write about it. What do two young boys do with dirty magazines and adult movies? I will let you ponder that for a moment. We should have never; I mean never had those materials, to begin with. We explored our sexuality and due to these encounters, I became confused at a young age about my own sexuality. I will not go into any further detail about this except to say these encounters were before puberty but it was detrimental to me and most likely to my friend for years to come.

Pornography though is a never-ending spiral of deception that has no end. It brings forth shame and regret and a very wrong perception of sex. I struggled with that addiction for decades and the only time it subsided was later when I had a girlfriend in my life and was having sex regularly.

Since this was my biggest addiction, I will start with this one. After my friend and I stopped because we were both feeling confused and that it was not right. My focus at this time was to just be a kid, heading into my teenage years. I was in church and went through confirmation at the age of thirteen. During this time, I did normal kid stuff, riding bikes, playing with my dog and I had my paper route for one of the local papers.

I was also really into baseball as it was about the only way my dad and I could connect. He was an avid Atlanta Braves fan as he had watched and listened to them growing up as a kid when they were the Milwaukee Braves, so naturally, I too was a Braves fan.

The seeds had been planted though; I had had a taste of tobacco, alcohol, and pornography, all before being a teenager.

There was a year of transition between thirteen and fourteen though. Drastic changes happened; as puberty had completely hit me by then, my body was being transformed. I got my first weight bench at fourteen and started lifting with my new best friend. The same young man that shared marijuana with me. I also had a rekindled friendship that year with another boy I had been friends with in elementary school. He lived behind me in the neighborhood and we rode bikes together often.

Things had changed but this was only the beginning. My sexual addiction started with the exposure to the materials that I already mentioned. However, being fourteen years old and in a small town, I was not able to get my hands on any new material myself. Being an underage adolescent, I found other avenues to go down. I would buy swimsuit magazines whenever I could, sexy posters from the local record store. I became friends with the man that ran the store while in junior high and through high school. It was a local shop that had records, tapes, CDs, comics, and posters.

As a teenager before we moved out to the country. We lived in a two-story house with sliding glass doors in the den on the first floor. My mother had an old-style sewing machine with a hideaway feature. It looked like a desk when the machine was put away. I had a small black binder where I hid the only pornography that I had at the time. It was a small catalog or magazine of sexual content. It was an odd size about that of a 5" by 7" photo. I used to hide it in the sewing machine, as my mother rarely used the machine. I used to sneak out at night and do immature pranks with my teenage friends. The usual toilet paper antics or other juvenile behavior that you would expect from teenage boys back in the 1980s.

Once I turned eighteen, however, it was full speed ahead. We had moved and were now living out in the country on a five-acre lot of land. I had a subscription to Playboy while living at home but I would also go out and buy all the adult magazines that I could. I will not list them here but back in the late 1980s, there was plenty to choose from. This was before the age of the Internet, so at that time almost anything you wanted was available in print. Sex sells even more so today than it did back then. Things are way worse in that aspect largely due to the Internet. Now, any kind of depravity you can think of is a keystroke away. Children are being exposed to this stuff at earlier and earlier ages all the time.

The current public education system in this country wants to indoctrinate kindergartners about homosexuality, transgender ideas and teach them sex education. I could write an entire chapter on this topic; however, I will keep it simple and say that when I was in elementary school the last thing on my mind was sex. I did not even know what sex was, nor should any five or six-year-old child. They are children and need to enjoy their childhood! Public officials should be ashamed of themselves and their outrageous behavior. Children are supposed to have an age of innocence and they are taking it away with these kinds of actions, day-by-day, and year-by-year.

Because our sex-driven society fed into my addiction, I feel the need to talk about pre-marital sex and what it does to people. As a typical teenager who was not walking in truth, I was bombarded on a daily basis with advertising of all sorts.

On television, in movies, and in music with most content about people having sex. It was normalized and it was something that almost all of your friends expected you to do. Of course, there was boasting and lying or severely stretching the truth by young boys. I am sure most of these escapades that we talked about only ever happened in our imagination. Not just boys but girls talk about this stuff too; actually, some of them seemed to have dirtier minds than the boys at the time.

I had a couple of girlfriends in my early teenage years, one at fourteen, another at sixteen. Then I went to a vocational school and met my first love or puppy love, as we were both very young. I was seventeen and she was close to my age, we dated for nine months in my junior year. She was sexually experienced and had a child that was about one and a half years old when we dated

She had her daughter at fifteen; she had been with a slightly older young man who had moved away. He had had some trouble with the law and left the area. I don't remember when precisely but she is whom I lost my virginity to. I was seventeen and excited about my newfound sex life. We had to sneak around and find places to park. She lived in the town where the school was and I was in my hometown about twenty miles away.

Not only was I having sex way before I should have but we were also parking here and there in the country and several times were interrupted by a police officer on patrol. We were young and in lust. I thought it was love but what did I know. Then one night, I was driving from her town on a road I had been on many times and was familiar and comfortable with. I was driving too fast for the conditions as it was raining, almost freezing rain in late December 1988.

We drove up over a small bridge that was over a ditch, there was a seam where the road met the slightly elevated bridge, and the car hydroplaned. We became airborne, I remember seeing a huge utility pole to my left and thick woods to my right. I attempted to steer to the left to take my chances with the pole and failed.

According to my girlfriend, I blacked out, we hit the pole, the car flipped and we got thrown out of the vehicle. Neither of us was buckled in. She was awake through the whole ordeal. When I came to, I was on the ground in extreme pain. My left shoulder was hurting badly. The weight of my entire body came down on it when I hit the ground. The people's yard we crashed in had come out to help us and put us in their garage on a concrete floor until the paramedics arrived. If God had not intervened, I could have been dead this very night. It was not my time nor was it my girlfriend's time to die. Many lessons came from this experience, including a spiritual flash or vision while I was out cold that lead to my first tattoo.

Chapter 3 Takeaway: Avoiding Sexual Sin

Pornography was introduced into my life at a young age.
I then developed a wrong view of sex as God had created and intended it to be.
Do you view sex and marriage as it is written in the Bible?

Bible verses to reflect upon:
Genesis 2:18, 24
I Corinthians 6:15-20

Chapter 4

Summer Sadness

A strange thing happened to me after my junior year of high school. What had been a year of my first love turned into a season of agony as she broke up with me before school let out for the summer. We had dated only nine months but this was the young lady I lost my virginity to. I was crushed. That summer I was seventeen and fell harder into drinking and smoking both cigarettes and marijuana. I spiraled out of control and left home for a short while, living in my car.

I was a complete mess. Eventually, I had to go back home and try to focus on the coming school year. I had my so-called friends that I was hanging out with; it was all usury as I look back on these events many years later. There would be one person having enough money to purchase marijuana then being pressured to share it with his friends. I was that person on more than one occasion.

It was early fall and school had started back up. One day after school as we were driving around in my car, and an argument broke out between me and this other friend. There were three of us in my car at the time. Do you know what the argument was about? He wanted me to smoke the last of my marijuana with him and my so-called best friend at the time. He got so mad, that he wanted to fight but I did not. I tried my best to talk with him but it was to no avail.

We were out driving around or cruising as they called it, then we decided to go to a secluded spot and get out of my vehicle to fight. This was not what I wanted but my so-called best friend at the time was a close friend with the other friend and he stirred the pot, so to speak. It was not much of a fight, the other friend made contact twice, and on that second hit to the face, I went down in the worst way possible.

I fell backward, twisting my leg, and snapped both bones completely. They took me to the local hospital in my car while I was in agonizing pain. Both of the bones, the tibia and fibula had snapped in half just above the ankle. I do not recall much after that. I know they took me (nurses or orderlies) to a room and that I had to be transferred to a hospital in the closest city. The local hospital for years has been called the band-aid station, as they could not handle anything serious.

I remember my father being furious with my so-called best friend for driving my car around for days and then bringing it back to the house with an empty fuel tank. I don't remember anything about being transferred to the hospital across the state line to Indiana. I do recall that I was laid up in that particular hospital for three days and they did nothing. I recall being in a great deal of pain and that they barely kept me medicated.

My older sister was a pharmacist at the time and worked at another hospital in the same city. She was furious about my situation and arranged a transfer for me to her hospital to be cared for. Once there, I was prepped for surgery and they put two screws in my leg because the break was so bad, they thought this would help it to set better. They put me in a thigh cast that came up high and kept my knee straight. It was just short of my groin. This was done to keep my leg from moving. We were now into school and the fall season; things were about to get interesting.

Chapter 4 Takeaway: Stay in the Word

I had gone through a season of depression because I was not focused on God.
How can you keep your eyes on the Lord?

Bible verses to reflect upon:
Isaiah 41:10
Matthew 11:28

Chapter 5

Compounding Addictions

The days of the thigh cast were interesting ones as I do not remember much about school during that time, only that I earned the nickname "part-timer" as I missed about seventy days of my senior year but because of my medical condition I did just barely pass and graduated that next summer.

I was on pain medication at the time that consisted of Percocet or Percodan and then to top it off with the other drug addictions that I had; I would drink. "Do not drink alcohol" with this drug is all I needed to see. A few beers or a little wine on top of these pills and I felt great. Thus, further feeding my addictions. I was not aware of the dependency that I was creating at the time.

My parents got me a used hospital bed to set up in the den of our home. The den was attached to the garage, so it was the first room you could enter from there. There was also a back door that led to our spacious backyard and the pond that we had way in the back. We had two televisions at the time, one large console in the front living room, and a smaller one in the den. I spent many hours in bed watching it, as with the large cast I could not do much of anything else.

One day, my best friend at the time, the one who was driving the car on that fateful day, came over and brought me something. It was called microdot or LSD (Lysergic acid diethylamide) in a tiny little pill. I remember him telling me to just have fun with it and that I would laugh a lot. I had no idea what I was doing. It was so tiny, like a piece of a broken pencil tip. I also had the thought of what can it do? It's so small. My mother was home and my sister was either at school or over at a friend's house.

I remember laughing profusely at the TV, just watching comedy shows and movies. I was laughing so much; my mother came in and checked on me to see what was going on. I was tripping pretty hard from what I remember as it was my first trip. Tripping is a term used to describe taking LSD, as it is a powerful drug that lasts 8 to 10 hours, you cannot make it stop, you have to let it run its course. It is a very dangerous drug because it is man-made, you never know who made it or how much of the drug you are going to get and it is illegal for these reasons. I don't recall anything else from that day.

I do know that later on, I wound up driving here and there in the cast. That was being creative. I would hobble out on my crutches and get in the car. I drove an old Mercury Cougar at the time and I would have to put my right leg that was in the cast over onto the passenger side floor area and drive with my left leg. This amazed my few friends at the time that I was able to do this. I ventured out here and there as I would go stir-crazy lying-in bed. The cast was so big and cumbersome that there was no possible way for me to attend school. I was attending vocational school taking electricity courses at the time. We had lesson time and shop time, but I was homebound in my condition.

One evening that fall, I was headed out of town on a local highway. It was raining slightly and foggy at the time. There was a dairy farm just as you were leaving town and you were able to accelerate your speed from 35 mph to 55 mph. It was also just after rounding a curve in the road. The unthinkable happened, I hit a cow. How did this happen? There was a whole herd of cows crossing the highway in the dark, misty fog. I was lucky I only hit one. I remember going back to the ranch and blowing the horn to get the farmer's attention. Remember, I am in this large leg cast.

The man that owned the ranch also went to the church I had been raised in. So, he knew who I was and I told him what happened. He went to go check on the cows and make sure nothing else happened. It turns out, one of his ranch hands did not secure the cattle gate in the afternoon at closing time and they got out. The cow survived; it had a slight leg injury. I hit the side of it, and there was cow poop all down the backside of my car. I forgot about this incident until at a family get-together years later when my youngest sister brought it up. Remember, hitting that cow?

Chapter 5 Takeaway: Have a Sound Mind

I did not have a sound mind during this time and made poor decisions.
How do you keep your mind focused on God?

Bible verses to reflect upon:
Isaiah 26:3-4
Colossians 3:2

Chapter 6

Demonic Visitors

I don't remember exactly when this event happened but it was while I was a senior in high school. It was after my thigh-high leg cast was removed and I was in a walking cast. One night I was laying in my twin bed, which was beside the outer wall and there was a window that was right about in the middle of where my bed sat. To give you a layout of my room at the time, also along that wall was a dresser that was a family antique that I had. On the adjacent wall was an old console television. The kind they used to make; a wooden floor model. Then I had a guitar amp and some speakers set up for my stereo.

I remember going to sleep and upon waking up I could not move. To be specific, I could only move my eyes to look around the room. This is commonly called sleep paralysis. Upon waking, there were three demons in my room. There was one between my bed and the dresser. This is the first one that I saw because of his size. I will say he was standing but he was so tall he was hunched over as he was standing there laughing at me. He had small wings and they did not accommodate his massive body. He most likely was eight feet tall as we had seven-foot ceilings and his head would have been in the attic if standing upright. He had yellow teeth, eyes, and fingernails. He was massive in size as a large bodybuilder. His skin was green and scaly. When he exhaled his breath, it was a yellow smoke-like vapor. There was an overpowering smell of sulfur in the room.

The second demon was much smaller, maybe four feet tall. He was small in appearance but he had the same physical characteristics as the large demon. He too had wings but they fit his body like he could have used them. The third demon was creepy in the aspect of it was a bust, like a statue. It was sitting on my television and was simply a head and upper torso, traditional bust style. It was sitting in the dark and I could not make out its features, but it turned its head to let me know it was alive.

The large demon was very close to me, as he was at the foot of my bed and was so large, I got a real good look at him. The second demon that was smaller was standing to the left side of the bed and was probably close to my knees where he was standing. He too was laughing at me. What happened next? I could not move and I could barely breathe. There was a crushing weight on my chest. As these demons were laughing and mocking me in my bedroom, I did the only thing I knew to do. I closed my eyes and whispered Jesus, Jesus, Jesus. This was all I could do; I could barely get those words out of my mouth. When I opened my eyes back up, the demons were gone and I could move.

Looking back on this event, I recall very clearly what happened. This was a result of what I had done a few years earlier when I spoke a curse from that satanic book that I had borrowed from my friend. I had opened a door into the darkness. That door was so dark that I chose to close it, remember? At least I thought I had.

There is something that I want you to understand. If you dabble with witchcraft as Hollywood has glamorized it over the last twenty years, as with the art of spells. You have an open door in your life that the enemy can come in with. One thing I learned by being in a Pentecostal church for seven years is there are many ways for Satan to have an inroad into your life.

If you are engaged in witchcraft, casting spells or tarot cards, seeing physics or mediums. These all have to do with conjuring up spirits. Ouija boards, horoscopes, and yoga are also open doors. Some of you may be saying, yoga?

Through the years, I have been in many automobile accidents and most of them were not my fault, getting hit in the rear of the vehicle I was driving or what they called being T-boned as well. I have had some serious injuries that I have had to work through and have therapy for. Through this process, I discovered yoga. I did yoga for stretching and some strengthening. I looked into going deeper and it just did not feel right. Why is that?

Later when I got into a Bible-believing and preaching church, the truth came out. Yoga stems from Eastern mysticism. Some even call it white witchcraft. If you find yourself in a group, perhaps in nature or at a fitness gym and you are all making the sound "ohm" you are opening a door. The enemy can walk right through this open door. You can look up yoga and witchcraft and you will find much information on the subject. You also have to be careful with meditation, which is a key element of yoga. It is, however, good to meditate on the Word of God.

There is also the thought in this country from a popular film series that has mainstreamed the use of good witchcraft to battle bad witchcraft as a good thing. This is normalizing witchcraft, a behavior or agenda of Hollywood.

Chapter 6 Takeaway:
Winning Spiritual Battles

I had previously opened the door to the enemy of my life and he came right in.
How do you close the doors to the enemy in your life?

Bible verses to reflect upon:
Isaiah 11:2
Ephesians 6:10-18

Chapter 7

Chemical Addictions

You may not understand if you have never partaken in these things but as a young man, I thought I could keep things from my parents. Smoking is the first one that I must tell you about. Have you ever smoked then quit? It doesn't take you long to notice how bad it smells and how it clings to your hair and clothes just being around someone who smokes. I picked up this addiction in the mid-1980s when cigarette machines were available in restaurants and hotels! Do you know or remember when? You would put cash into these machines and pull a knob to get the brand that you wanted. This was at least a decade before the debit card came out in the mid-1990s. These machines were expensive but you could get your smokes, no questions asked if you timed it just right.

I also had a friend who worked at a full-service gas station at the time. I became friends with his manager there as well and it was an easy way to get cigarettes. They also became marijuana friends, as we would later get high together. In the 1980s there was no legal marijuana anywhere in the US, it was illegal in all 50 states. I am sure many of you know how bad cigarettes are for you with all the chemicals, tar, and nicotine they have. It is a very divisive product that once it has its hooks in you, can be almost impossible to put down. I smoked from age fourteen to twenty-four and at my worst was smoking two packs a day in college in the early 1990s.

Between cigarettes and marijuana, I was wrecking my body and did not even realize it until it started to affect my vocals. I was playing guitar and singing at the time when I noticed a change and struggle with my voice. I liked marijuana so much at the time; I decided to just quit cigarettes. It took me a little while and this was before the patch or any of those help you to quit smoking products came out. This was before big tobacco was exposed and went on their massive apology ad campaign as well. I started out by smoking less and using marijuana as a crutch to help me quit cigarettes. I went from two packs to a single pack to half a pack to about four or five cigarettes a day when I finally quit. My biggest craving was after eating, especially a full meal.

I became tobacco-free but still had two gorillas on my back. A term people like to say is that they have a monkey on their back when it comes to addictions. Mine were gorillas and they were marijuana and alcohol. I had quit smoking cigarettes in 1994 and would not stop my marijuana usage until 1998 when I was attending my second college after being determined to make a change.

With marijuana, I got high for the first time at fourteen and quit at twenty-six, so about twelve years of use with this drug. I say drug because that is what it is, for the longest time I argued that it was a plant and why it should be legal. Now, almost twenty-five years later all but six states have legalized either medical or recreational marijuana or a combination of both. That is a staggering statistic and it will only be a matter of time before the federal government changes its stance on the subject as well. I am not a proponent of the drug because I know how detrimental it can be.

You may be wondering why do people do the things they do? Smoke, drink and use drugs, and a whole list of other things. It's called escapism. Simply wanting to forget your surroundings, who you are, what your troubles are and what you are facing in reality. You know the space we all live in? This was my problem; I did not like my surroundings and I did these things to escape them.

My other big-time addiction was alcohol. Ever hear the words Wine and Spirits? It is advertised that way in most towns and cities wherever alcoholic beverages are sold.

There is some truth in advertising after all! How about demon alcohol? There is a reason for these terms for this drug that has been around for thousands of years. It lowers your guard, dulls your senses, and makes you susceptible to suggestions. Society has separated this by putting the labels out there of drugs and alcohol. It is all the same and this drug kills almost 90,000 people annually by abuse alone. Where did I begin with this one? At age nine in a barn, drinking a can of beer.

This addiction crept in on me. I mean at the time I had limited access to the stuff. My dad kept beer on hand and almost all of my friend's dads did as well. We would sneak a beer here or there but this one did not take off until I got my license and was able to drive. Driving was a freedom that led to going to other people's houses and on occasion getting an adult to buy beer for us. That's something that is called contributing to the delinquency of a minor and is a crime. By the time I was seventeen, my best friend and I at the time were smoking cigarettes, getting high on marijuana, and drinking when we could. I went from beer to wine and back again. I dabbled with hard liquor here and there but that was a tall order for us back then. We also did not want to lose our faculties completely and get busted for drunk driving or by whoever parent's house we were at, at the time.

One of the worst experiences I ever had, was one night my best friend and I were out driving around smoking marijuana and drinking wine. My friend had purchased some marijuana that was laced with Formaldehyde. We knew it was embalming fluid but we were young and reckless. My friend got sick, all down the side of the car as we were driving along. I was nauseous myself but did not vomit. I remember taking him home and having to hose the side of the car off. The things we do to ourselves when we are engaged in the drug culture.

I got into trouble with the law before turning twenty-one. A couple of these older guys I was friends with bought liquor, wine, and marijuana. We went out partying and did some really stupid stuff. What do you do in a small town that has only a few bars and hardly anything for kids to do? Young adults at the time but still, the one theater we had when I was a young boy went out of business and we only had a bowling alley. That was about it, no real activities to do unless you were involved in sports, which I was not. So, when we were out drinking, these guys and I went and committed some acts of vandalism. What we did angered the community and a reward was offered for any information leading to our arrest. Yes, it was that bad. In the end, we were turned in, arrested, and convicted.

This was the first hard lesson that I learned with alcohol that would eventually keep me sober for three years. I was a young adult, old enough to go into the military but not old enough to drink. There were many things I had to go through during this period. I had been sentenced but received probation, as this was my first real trouble with the law. I had to attend Alcoholics Anonymous classes that seemed to go on forever.

What I recall from those days is this, back then people could smoke in buildings, and boy did they. The group that I was assigned to, so to speak, was in the next town over. They were chain-smoking, coffee-drinking addicts. They had exchanged one addiction for two more, Nicotine and Caffeine. I drank caffeinated drinks for decades, so I am not casting stones here but these people were hard-core users of these two substances.

The other thing that I recall was; I had to say "Hi I'm Shane and I'm an alcoholic" Everyone had to say this phrase with his or her name at the start of every meeting. This bothered me; I was nineteen at the time and had the thought that these people are stuck in a holding pattern. Some of these people had been attending meetings for three times a day for ten years or longer. Sadly, some had never moved ahead with the fact that they had quit drinking and still identified themselves as an alcoholic, even if it had been decades since they had quit drinking.

There is one other thing that I remember about attending those meetings at that particular location. If you were a regular attendee at a specific meeting and missed for whatever reason the people there would question you and make you feel guilty for not being there. These were court-appointed sessions, so the chairperson who was in charge of the meeting had to sign my sheet with the date and time to acknowledge that I had been there. When I was done with all of my court-appointed meetings, I decided that this path was not for me. I will say the organization has helped millions of people to get sober and that is a good thing.

Chapter 7 Takeaway: Be Sober

Being driven by the flesh was how I was living my life with many addictions.
How can you be more mindful of the things of God?

Bible verses to reflect upon:
Isaiah 5:11
I Peter 5:8-9

Chapter 8

Young Love

During this time, I had a girlfriend who later became my first fiancé. I met her when I was a senior and she was sophomore, it was springtime. We started out simply as friends and would just hang out with one another.

This was shortly before I got into my legal troubles. I later took her to both of her junior and senior proms even though I was fresh out of high school. We had a long relationship for the time and for the ages that we were, it lasted almost three years. We did many things together, including smoking marijuana. However, that all changed when I got into trouble. Part of my conviction for the vandalism crime included a thirty-day jail sentence at the county jail. As mentioned previously, the town was outraged by this particular act of vandalism and I believe the presiding judge wanted people to see that there was real jail time.

I went at the appointed time and turned myself in, in those days they allowed me to do this because I was living at home and was not a flight risk. This was an old-time county jail. There was a small mess area with tables, a payphone, and a television. You could play cards, eat meals, make collect calls and watch television at certain times.

One of the first nights I was there, I was on the payphone with my girlfriend. I remember her being upset that we could not be together and she could not come to see me without a parent because she was under the age of eighteen at the time. We were talking on the phone and I am sure that phone went to a recorder before being sent out to the recipient. This was a jailhouse payphone. During the call, she cried and was upset and I kept assuring her that somehow, someway I would be with her that night.

I knew I was in a concrete and steel jail and would not be going anywhere in the physical sense. We finished talking and I went to my cot back in the cell area to lie down and go to sleep. I prayed and I prayed. I really wanted to be with her as she was so upset that we could not see one another or be with each other. Something happened that night that I have carried with me ever since.

I was in the top bunk and I closed my eyes. I went to sleep and I awoke, almost in an instant. Something was very different though. I was floating towards the ceiling and looked back at my body, which was asleep and still breathing. I had no idea what was happening except for I was separated from my body. I floated up from my cot, through the ceiling, and into the attic area of the jail. I then continued to float upwards through the roof and into the night air.

I knew I was not dead, as I saw my body asleep and breathing. I was in this small town and my girlfriend lived by the state line on the very outskirts of the same county. I headed out and flew in that direction. I was a hundred or so feet off of the ground and by instinct; I followed the local highway out of town. I remember the trees down below as I drifted slightly upward and looked out and up towards the stars. Then I passed the woman's house that used to cut my hair when I was a boy. That was about the last thing that I saw. It was night, it was dark and I was flying through the air headed towards my girlfriend's house.

The next thing I know, I am coming back from the other state and approaching her house from the opposite direction. I do not recall how fast I was going or how far I traveled. I could have been traveling thousands of miles per hour. One minute, I was by a house I knew very well and the next minute I had completely missed my girlfriend's house by many miles. I approached the house, still in the air, and traveled through the roof into her bedroom. She was in her bed sound asleep. I got into bed with her, snuggled up beside her, and went to sleep. When I awoke the next morning, I was back in jail.

What happened? This had been an actual and fully detailed out-of-body experience. I believe God answered my prayer and allowed me to experience this to prepare me for the things that were going to come my way.

Chapter 8 Takeaway: Seeking Help From God

I had made some mistakes and was asking for something special from God.
God is faithful through it all, including our troubles if we seek Him.
How do you seek Him in your time of need?

Bible verses to reflect upon:
Jeremiah 17:7-8
John 14:1

Chapter 9

Walking the Straight Line

When I was released from jail, the probation portion of my sentence took effect. I remember not taking this seriously or thinking that I was smart enough to fake it. That is exactly what I did, as I continued to keep drinking even though I was under the age of twenty-one. I should have taken this seriously after being in the local jail for thirty days but did not and the long arm of the law caught up with me once again. This time, I violated probation with additional alcohol charges.

I had been arrested and had to face the reality that I was always trying to escape. My probation officer was not happy with me at all and gave me a stone-cold choice. I could either enter rehabilitation to get clean and sober or go to prison. I would have had to serve my original sentence for the vandalism crime. I realized now that I had to actually be clean and sober because of the probation, urine tests, and the genuine possibility of going to prison.

I chose a rehabilitation canter a few towns over from where I was living. Being in a small town there was no such place for treatment. Here I go again, round two of the dreaded alcohol game. It was only by the grace of God that I did not have to go to prison. God had shown me His grace and mercy through this entire process.

What I remember most about the rehabilitation center was our group session. Many things occurred at the center, having single evaluations with therapists and people who had degrees in psychology. There was one particular group session that stands out to me, it was weekly on Saturdays and your immediate family came and attended it with you. Looking back at this, it was an embarrassing situation or perhaps more accurately a humbling experience for everyone who checked into the center.

You had to talk about what you had learned through your experience. Most of the people were there because of alcohol-related offenses, mainly drunk driving. You did share in your experience of why you were there and I do not recall anyone being there voluntarily but that was an available option at the center. What life actions were you going to do now that you were rehabilitated and knew all of the dangers of drinking alcohol and what it does to you?

Many people smoked in the building but when the group session was underway, they wanted people to not smoke. I remember many cigarette packs sitting on the long conference table that was actually several of the same size tables put together. You could smoke in the building, as this was the early 1990s. Shocking to think that today, people smoking in a building. I remember my mom, dad, and my youngest sister coming to that last group session. I was glad to put all this behind me and I did stop drinking. It is amazing what you can do when the thought of going to state prison is hanging over your head.

There was one gentleman that I knew from my hometown but he was the only one. The days were filled with one-on-one counseling sessions, small group sessions, and then the weekly large group session. At the time, I had a therapist who was actually kind of a sarcastic person but looking back on this I am sure he had his own problems.

My counselor had a full head of gray hair when I went there, yet the man could not have been forty years old at the time. I remember telling him, I was going to quit drinking, smoking, and caffeine. He would tell me one habit at a time, Shane. As with the Alcoholics Anonymous group many people also had a coffee habit, mine was soda at the time.

Previously, I had begun to let my hair grow out before all the legal trouble and the lawyer my family hired insisted that I have a clean-cut look. No facial hair and I had to cut my hair, to have it above the collar of my shirt. I did so at his insistence and afterward, during my time at the rehabilitation center I was so outspoken about growing my hair back and not cutting it for anyone, ever. This annoyed my counselor for some reason and he would be sarcastic towards me and with me at those times. I find it strange that this is what I remember most about him, looking back at my time in rehab.

I had successfully finished all courses and requirements through the rehabilitation program. Now it was time to put my life into action by remaining clean and sober. God's grace and mercy had brought me through a challenging time.

Chapter 9 Takeaway: Avoiding a Rebellious Attitude

I was still being driven by my flesh and only brought it into submission because of the law.
How do you stop the spirit of rebellion between you and God?

Bible verses to reflect upon:
Proverbs 12:21
I Peter 1:13-14

Chapter 10

Crossing State Lines

After rehabilitation, I had to walk that straight line. There was a strange set of circumstances that came up shortly thereafter. For one, my mom decided she was going to leave my dad and file for divorce after twenty-nine years of marriage. And two, my girlfriend at the time was having problems with her mom and step-dad and wanted to go live with her biological dad across the state line.

I remember, thinking I needed to leave and relocate, I did so legally with the permission of my probation officer. A transfer was set up and I just had to meet with my new probation officer each month. By this time, jail time had been served, court costs and fines had been paid and I think my first probation officer thought it was a good thing for me to move and get some new friends.

We were both young at the time and her dad was a regular guy by 1990s standards. He smoked cigarettes, drank beer regularly, worked full time, had a house and a couple of vehicles. She and I both smoked and did not have to hide it as her dad smoked as well.

We had a bedroom and that was it. Yes, we were living together and were sexually active in her dad's house. It is strange but the only time he seemed to be bothered by me was when I was in between one job or another. I went from job to job back in those days because I was young, immature, and had no idea what I wanted to do to earn an income. My dream was to be a traveling musician in a successful, label-signed band back then. However, that was a dream at that time and I had to have a real job making real money. Since we only had one bedroom, most of my belongings stayed at my parent's house. I had my clothes, guitar, and my car at the time. I even left my bed back home, as we did not need it. This was a strange time for me, as my mom was still at the house taking care of my sister and my dad was an over-the-road truck driver and was gone five to six days a week.

There came an opportunity to go back home after about six months of living at my girlfriend's father's house. I could not or did not want to hold a job consistently and I think he was honestly just tired of the situation. Maybe he grew a conscience? Knowing his oldest daughter was sexually active with me in his own house? Whatever the case, it was time to go back across the state line and reconnect with my former probation officer.

He was surprised and maybe shocked by this. At the time that I left to go live in the other state, my mom and dad were still under the same roof. This was after my mother had made it clear; she was filing for divorce and was going to leave my dad. While I was in the other state, things became too much at the house and my mother decided that she was moving out. She had also decided she was going to go to college, she was in her 40s at the time.

My dad had to continue working his job; he had a pension and had been with the company for almost thirty years at that point in his life. My dad offered to cover all living expenses if my girlfriend and I came back to the home I had left. This worked for a while, as my sister was fourteen to fifteen years old during this time. I can tell you we went to concerts together, my girlfriend and I would take my sister and her boyfriend to shows and we had a good time.

Things all came to end though around Christmas 1992. My fiancé decided to go back to her home with her mom and stepdad and broke it off with me. I was devastated again! For the second time in my young life, I was at a complete loss for what to do. My probation was finally over and I could move on but what was I going to do?

I decided to follow what I had looked at in high school before my leg broke in the worst way possible. That was going to an art school. After several weeks of mourning the relationship, we had been in for the last two and half years. I applied to go to an art school in another state.

I had time to spend just being myself, still living at home and watching over my youngest sister. After I applied and was accepted, I then planned a trip to go out and visit the college. My brother-in-law, who was married to my oldest sister, took a couple of days off from work and we drove out to stay in a hotel and visit the school and the surrounding area.

I remember being in the hotel and him asking me what I wanted to do. He drank, smoked cigarettes and marijuana. Previously, I had decided to go back to using marijuana after I got off of probation but my 21st birthday came and went as I was sober for almost two years and was not interested in drinking then. At that moment, however, I threw my sobriety away in one fell swoop. I felt like it was time to be me. I was twenty-one and legal to drink, so I resumed it. That was in the early spring and I was going to be attending classes in the summer.

It is a miracle that I did not get into any more trouble before leaving for college. I can tell you, even though I was drinking and smoking marijuana I wanted to make it to college and get out of my hometown.

One of the worst things that happened during those months was resentment from my dad towards me because I decided to leave. My mom was gone and attending college herself. She lived in the next town over and was going through her lifestyle changes after divorcing my dad.

My dad would end up making arrangements with one of our neighbors. That was one of my sister's best friends who lived close by to keep my sister through the week. Then my mom and her new boyfriend ended up helping out part of the time as well. That was incredibly awkward and not a good thing as my sister was fifteen at the time. I know this was hard on her emotionally. She had chosen to stay with my dad because of all the things my mother was going through and it was the only home she knew. She would have her driver's license that fall and my dad would buy her a car.

It was truly a bad situation all the way around but I was depressed after losing what felt like the love of my life. We had similar or some of the same friends and you know what made the break up even worse? I found out from those friends that my fiancé had not been faithful to me for quite some time. She was very promiscuous from what I was told at the time, with several people. I had to look back at some of the people and situations that were pointed out to me and realized that there was some truth there.

This just sent me over the deep end. I was on a path of self-destruction and I simply did not care. That was all the reason that I needed to leave. I felt like a fool in front of people that I thought were my friends and I even posed the question to at least one of them; why didn't you come and say something to me? The reply that I got made all the sense in the world then. Would you have believed me? Or would you have stood by your woman? I knew the answer, but it still did not take the sting away.

I thought my life there sucked and I was going to leave it behind and have that rock star music career with alcohol, drugs, and sex. I had a terrible mindset and was headed down the road of death and destruction.

One event stands out to me very clearly about death and near-death in particular. I was trading marijuana at the time to support my habit. One Saturday afternoon, I went to the other state to see friends, visit and smoke marijuana. At one of those stops, my friend of a friend's girlfriend wanted to come along as I traveled to see others. I was young, immature, and thought the best of people for the most part. We were gone several hours and when we got back to her place a terrible thing happened.

Her boyfriend, who was an acquaintance of mine through my ex-fiancé's dad was there and immediately took her into a bedroom and questioned her. He made me sit on the couch in the living room and when he came out, he was furious. The woman decided she would lie to make him jealous. Who knows what was going on in their relationship at the time? She told him that we kissed or made out.

He lost it and pulled out a small 22-caliber pistol and put it in my face. I mean it was an inch from my nose.

That happened three times, as I would dispute what she said and he would go back into the bedroom to question her again and again.

I was scared to move off of the couch. During one of those times, I was rubbing my arm where I have a couple of tattoos and he said "your tattoos aren't going to save you now". This was when tattoos were still kind of taboo and some people including myself thought they gave you a tough outer appearance.

I don't know what she said to him each time he went into that bedroom. I do know there were angels and demons present during this exchange. If he had pulled the trigger, I would have been dead and you would have never heard of this ministry or me. At least one angel was holding him back from pulling the trigger and a demon was telling him to pull it.

That man at the time, as I would later find out was incredibly high on powder cocaine during the exchange. There was also a couple living in the basement that I was a casual friend with at the time. They of course had heard the whole exchange as the man was screaming most of the time. They both came up from the basement and were naked; she had a pillow covering her front. She came over to me and whispered; "You need to leave now, while you can" I quietly and gently got up from the couch and headed out the front door. I got in my car and left. I thanked God all the way home that I was still alive and that He had spared my life this very night.

Chapter 10 Takeaway: Trusting God

I was on the wrong road and had opened the wrong door.
God's grace and mercy were upon me and He kept me from great tragedy.
How do you stay on the right path with God if danger confronts you?

Bible verses to reflect upon:
Psalms 46:1
I Peter 5:7

Chapter 11

The City Calls

The time had finally come and I was getting ready to move to the big city and leave my hometown that had been home to me most of my life. Sadly because of these events coming to fruition my dad and I did not talk and he resented that I was leaving to go to college at this particular time. He wanted me to wait until my sister was eighteen, which made sense, however, I do not believe he had any idea of how ashamed, embarrassed, foolish, heartbroken, and depressed I was. My fiancé had made a real fool of me and my so-called friends were just that.

The day came for the move, with a trailer attached to my dad's truck, my mom, her boyfriend, and myself all headed to the city. I had a passenger car at the time and drove separately as it was not equipped to tow anything. My mother was quite supportive of me during this time. She loved me as a mother would but she had just recently divorced my dad and was in college herself in her 40s. She was happy that I was getting away from the heartache of my last relationship and the tension at home that I was leaving behind, at least for now.

When we got to the city, I had a dorm room arranged through the college, as I knew absolutely no one there. My mom, her boyfriend, and I unloaded my belongings and to this day I have some pictures of her and me in a park from that weekend. It was a good weekend even with the uncertainty that was ahead of me. In my mind, I was starting a new chapter in my life.

It's funny how people will say things like I don't remember the 1970s as in a drug reference. I can tell you the next couple of years that were about to unfold would kind of be like that for me.

Living in the dorm was strange and interesting all at the same time. This was the early 1990s and the Internet was not something we had access to and it was certainly not a way of life as it is today. The first summer of classes I tried my best but I was also drinking daily, smoking cigarettes, and using marijuana whenever I could.

You all have an idea of what a frat house is like. Living in this dorm was just like that only it was on steroids because it was a coed dorm. Guys and girls were shacking up together or staying over consistently. There were drinking parties every night and marijuana was readily available. It was a free-for-all most days. I think in the beginning perhaps the dorms were monitored as to whom was living in them but that seemed to quickly fall to the wayside. The college made massive amounts of money by over occupancies in these rooms.

I had a room with two other guys. One guy and I shared the bedroom and the second guy had a hammock strung out in the living room-studio area. By any means, there should have been only two of us living in this dorm. This was common across the whole building, which was eight stories high and housed hundreds of students. It did not take long for us to realize the fact that was before us. I got along with those two guys and we had what I would say was an acceptable living arrangement between the three of us.

Then one day, my roommate decided he was moving out. He had found some friends that had rented a place off-campus and it was way more affordable than the dorm. The college was notified that he was leaving and his space opened up. His space happened to be in the bedroom we shared. We wound up getting another guy that my other roommate knew and so it was that the new guy moved in. I had ventured out by meeting people in my classes and by being one of the students who were fortunate enough to have a car.

I had made some new friends and to my surprise, they too lived in the suburbs and rented a large house together. I went out there on the weekends to hang out and party. That consisted of drinking and smoking marijuana. I had only been doing that for a few weeks and one Sunday, when I came back to my dorm I was shocked as to what had happened while I was away.

The first thing I saw was blood. It seemed like it was everywhere in streaks and drops. It was on the front door, on the floor, and all over the bathroom. This was late morning around lunchtime when I arrived back and asked my roommate what happened. He explained to me that our new roommate attempted suicide Saturday night over a girl. He said that our new roommate was all right and his cuts were minor, however, there was quite a bit of blood throughout our dorm. I was shocked and outraged by what had happened and by the fact that my roommate had not bothered to clean any of the blood up. We only had one bathroom.

I called my friend out in the suburbs and asked if there was any room that I could rent from them. I was angry and afraid that the new roommate of ours was mentally unstable and could not be trusted as he just tried to kill himself. I decided right then and there that I was done with this situation. My friend let me come stay and then we talked about the available room, bills, and the rules of the house. I agreed and we made arrangements to move my belongings in shortly afterward. This all happened in just a couple of days. Just like that and my dorm days were over.

Chapter 11 Takeaway: Helping Others

I was more concerned with my safety than that of my suicidal roommate who had his own addictions and demons.
How do you stand firm on the Word of God and witness to those in need?

Bible verses to reflect upon:
Psalms 91:1-10
2 Peter 3:9

Chapter 12

Party on

The roommate situation that was the final straw happened in August just before the fall semester was about to begin. Looking back at that time, I struggled to stay afloat with grades. Here I was in a new city, in a new state and I was doing what I wanted to do with college.

What was happening and I did not realize it; I was on the very slippery slope of chemical addiction. Remember, I had gone through rehabilitation and I thought, "I can handle this". I was able to for a while but the lifestyle kept creeping in. The first semester I was just above a 2.0 GPA or a C student. That is kind of crazy when you think about it. I mean here I was in college working towards my music and video business associate's degree. I wanted to do this, I chose to be here and this was a two-year college at the time.

I had finished my first semester but my grades would continue on a downward trend the next semester. I flunked a class. I was paying to be here and I flunked a class! The teacher and I did not get along. There was spiritual strife between us as he was a homosexual and I happened to dislike that lifestyle choice. That however is not why I flunked; I was a poor student in his class and in that subject. I did not adjust my habits though and the downward trend continued. It was now wintertime and I was in my third semester. Guess what happened?

That's right, I flunked another class with a different teacher. I will fall back on my previous assessment of being a poor student. I was entirely too focused on the party lifestyle. I was living in this beautiful French Victorian home in a wonderful suburb. We were all students or former students in the home. Some people could be social drinkers and do what needed to be done for school. I was not one of those people. I drank and smoked marijuana to escape my reality. This pattern of addiction continued with me even though I had left my hometown.

I was now living in a city, in a different state, going to college with like-minded people of my age, for the most part, and that was what I had wanted to do. Why was I getting poor grades and flunking classes? It was because of my attitude and my actions. Friends, when you are engaged in substance abuse it hinders you emotionally, physically, and spiritually.

I had gone back to drinking because my former fiancé broke my heart and I was in a bad place in all three of those areas. I did not care anymore and chose to do what I had previously known. Escapism, do these things and I won't feel the pain anymore? Being an alcoholic, drug addict, building up walls to keep people out. These are all self-destructive actions and attitudes.

I did have a wake-up moment for a brief period of time during all of this. I realized what was happening and I took the next semester off from all regular classes to focus on retaking the two classes that I had flunked. That was my best semester with a 3.4 GPA or B+ average. That would be the pinnacle of my grades at my first college. I felt great during that time as I felt I could apply myself. Then summer came, it had now been one year at the college and I was a semester behind. What happened?

That party lifestyle took center focus again. There is something else that happened during this time. I lived in this large house with nine other people and there were musicians in the home. A band came together and I started to help out with them as a roadie for their local gigs. Those guys were all students at the college, had part-time jobs, and were working on music as well. I wanted to be a part of the music lifestyle, so I helped out as a roadie.

We had parties at least once a month and invited many people to come out to the house. There are two of these house parties that were life-altering events for me. One was spiritual and the other was physical.

I will start with the spiritual event that happened. We were in full party mode but the scene was not out of hand. People were drinking, smoking cigarettes, and just conversing with one another. We had a big house with a grand wooden staircase. There was the basement; the first floor and then most of the bedrooms were on the second and third floors. A friend of mine and I were sitting on the stairs in the foyer area of the first floor.

I do not recall who gave me the LSD but it was the paper version of the drug. It was a tiny square with the drug on it; which was originally in liquid form. This was the most common form of the drug back then. What I did not realize until afterward was that it was called "windowpane" because it was not one dose of the drug but four doses in one. This is a dangerous, powerful and illegal drug because of just that and many other reasons. I am thankful that my friend was sitting with me because the house was full of strangers. Many people I did not know but my roommates did. So what happened?

I remember looking at him and we both agreed we were very high. He had done the drug too and we were feeling the same. Immediately after this, I left my body. I mean, I floated towards the front door, looked back, and saw myself sitting on the stairs with my friend. Remember my out-of-body experience when I was in jail? It was exactly like that, except I had not prayed to God for this but had done an illegal drug instead. It was intense and could have gone very wrong. I stopped at the door and realized if I chose to leave, that was it. My life as I knew it, may be all over. I went back to my body and floated downward into it. As soon as I was back in my body, I thought I have got to go outside and get some air.

I want to share something with you here. What I realized at the door was, I could have become one of those people who went into a vegetative state. I knew of someone in my extended family when I was a young child that took their own life and it was blamed on this drug. That person was never the same and was committed to a mental ward and then finally took their own life. I remembered that and chose to go back to my body. Friends, this is a very dangerous drug and there are unpredictable things that can happen to you.

When I went outside, I was speeding my butt off with the high I was on. I had to talk to myself, out in the yard to keep it together. There was a young couple getting beer from the keg on the back porch and I remember them talking about me, thinking I was out of mind. They had no idea how close to being right they were. It is only by the grace of God that I kept it together that night.

Just a few weeks later, we were all at it again. I will be completely transparent with you here. At that point in my young life, I thought I would be dead by the age of thirty. I frankly did not care about myself in any way, shape, or form at that point. The drugs, alcohol, and my lifestyle were going to kill me.

That is when the first real wake-up call hit. We were having another party and it was the weekend of my birthday. The band was playing in the basement and it was full-on party mode. That was a suburban neighborhood and even though the band was in the basement, it was loud and people were coming and going. The police were called; I had to talk to them. There was a noise complaint and we actually had a paper sign up at the front door charging a cover fee. That was to cover the cost of the beer kegs and to give money to the band. The police said that we could not charge money as we were not a licensed establishment and this was a residential neighborhood. They made me take down the sign and warned me that we had to quiet down, as they did not want to come back here on another call. No one listened and they came back.

The police performed a raid of the house without a search warrant. They stormed the house, drove people out, and arrested a few people including myself. Unfortunately for me, I had drugs in my possession. This was the beginning of the end of my college days, my use of heavy drugs, and the realization that I may be facing prison time, again. The party was over.

Chapter 12 Takeaway: Relying on God

In my most desperate time of need, I turned back to God in prayer. I had made many bad decisions on my own, driven by the flesh. Do you ask God for guidance in the challenges that you face?

Bible verses to reflect upon:
Psalms 18:2
Philippians 4:6

Chapter 13

Reality Check

There is nothing like being arrested, booked, and locked into a community cell or what some used to call the drunk tank. I had done it this time and was uncertain of what was to come. Looking back at this event I remember clearly one thing. There was an angel that spoke to me; only I did not listen when clear direction was given. When the police returned to the house for the second time, I was downstairs and could have easily hidden the money and drugs that I had on me. I was told to put those things away. I was high on LSD and did not listen.

If the police ever raid your house, you will sober up quickly regardless of what drugs you may be on. At least I did. You may think, well you were high; you probably thought you heard that. No, I heard it plain as day and I did not listen. When I went upstairs, it only took a few seconds for me to be accosted by a police officer. It was all over now. I had several hundred dollars, illegal drugs, and paraphernalia on me when I was arrested. That was not good at all, if I would have listened to the angel, I may have been arrested but would not have been facing the charges that I was about to be.

I had a roommate who unfortunately had a bad crack cocaine habit that I was unaware of. He had been away the night of the party and when I phoned home the next day, he answered and I asked him to get what cash I had in the house and if he had to, go and pawn one of my guitars to get me out of jail. My roommate's addiction came to light during this process. I have no way of knowing how much money he received for pawning my nicest guitar at the time. It seems he pawned a few other things as well and this shocked me. I overlooked that but questioned within myself how much money did he actually receive? I did not care though as I was thankful to be out of jail

Once I was out, I went to class at the college and confided in a teacher about being arrested for drug possession and thankfully they knew of a lawyer that would most likely defend me. I will simply say that God was intervening in my life and showing me grace and mercy despite my carelessness.

As things proceeded that fall and winter, I finally had to withdraw or you could say I flunked out and dropped out all at the same time. With the pending case, police surveillance, and the pressure of what I was facing, I was a mess. I drank; smoked cigarettes and my friends disappeared or drastically distanced themselves from me. When you are in the drug culture and you get arrested for drug possession, bad things can and do happen.

I had lost all but my closest friends due to my arrest. Thankfully, the police made a big mistake in their eagerness to break up our college party that was out of hand. Through the process of hiring a criminal lawyer, when he discovered that the police had come to the house already, then left and came back without a search warrant and did what they did. Frankly, they did not have a case.

They had also broken a side gate leading to the backyard during the raid and that was brought up before the judge in my defense effort. This never went to a full trial and was only ever before a judge who passed a sentence on much lesser charges. Now, I had to pay full court costs and was on probation for six months. That was to ensure that I paid the city all of the money I owed them.

I moved out of the party house when all of this was done and stayed with one of my musician friends. Things just did not work out though and I had to face the inevitable fact that it was time to go back home.

Other things happened during this time that God brought me through. The rock and roll lifestyle nearly killed me, cost me friends, and alienated me from people that I thought were my friends. Now

I would head back to my hometown with only my true best friend, my canine companion whom I rescued from the pound, also known as dog jail.

Chapter 13 Takeaway: God's Direction

In an instant, my life was forever changed and I prayed for God's will to be done.
Do you pray for God's will to be done in your life?

Bible verses to reflect upon:
Psalms 138:7
Romans 8:28

_____
_____
_____
_____
_____
_____
_____
_____
_____
_____
_____
_____
_____

Chapter 14

Going Home

I don't recall the drive back home. I was depressed, defeated, and felt like a failure. What had been an aspiration, dream, and desire of mine just a few years earlier, now felt like the smoldering ashes from a once-mighty fire. I did not have a good relationship with my dad at the time and it did not help my situation. I had crashed and burned and was at an even lower point than when I had left to go to college. How was this possible?

I was not focused on God at all. Oh, I prayed and prayed often with the legal trouble that I had been facing but I was not living for God. I was caught up in all of my own fleshly desires and satisfying my carnal lusts. My oldest sister took me in and had compassion for me. My brother-in-law who had gone with me a few years earlier to explore the city was receptive as well. He and I had some of the same habits, cigarettes, marijuana, and alcohol.

Shortly after moving in with them, I woke up one morning and had incredible pain in my low back. My sister and brother-in-law were both at work and the kids were in school, so I was home alone. The pain got worse minute by minute. I called my mom, who lived in town, and thankfully she was available and came out to get me. The pain was so bad; I had to lay face down on the floor. What was happening?

I did not know except the lower right side of my back felt like someone was wringing it out like a sponge. My mother arrived and I got up and went out to her car. She knew I was in really bad pain and I needed to go to a hospital. She drove towards the local hospital and was going to turn in. I looked at it and then to her and told her to drive on. She was concerned and asked me if I was sure, I said yes. As I remembered, that facility could not handle my broken leg back in high school and had earned the nickname of the band-aid station throughout our town. She drove on, across the state line to that nearest city, where I had previously been for my leg surgery and we went into an emergency room.

It was discovered that I had a large kidney stone that had just made it out of the kidney and was stuck in my back. I mean to tell you, this was excruciating pain. It was intense, terrible pain. The doctor said we will take care of this. He said " We're going to have to blast it with ultrasound. " For a moment, I thought "blast?"

They had me lay on a cold stainless steel table. Then they lathered a lubricant on my stomach and used a strong ultrasound to blast the stone into many tiny pieces. It felt very strange to me but he did not stop until my back felt better. That meant that he had successfully destroyed the stone and then he gave me the other news.

What was that, you ask? The nurse came in and handed me a funnel with a built-in strainer. For the next two weeks, I had the task of urinating through this special funnel to collect those tiny fragments. It did not take a full two weeks but instead was about ten days of this.

Once all those tiny fragments were collected, my mother and I went back for my check-up and to turn in the fragments for testing. Exactly three weeks to the day of the first kidney stone attack there was a second. I could not believe it. The doctor had questioned my health choices at the time including all aspects of my diet. I don't recall how much of that set in with me but after what I was about to go through, I did make some changes for the better. I will keep this as polite as possible. The stone had come around to the front of my body. It was stuck in the very lower part of my pelvic area. It was stuck in my urinary tract. I asked the doctor quite plainly if he was going to blast it with ultrasound again. To my surprise, he said, "no, I am going to fish it out."

Yes, it sounds as bad as it was for me. He took a tube and some kind of surgical string and went in through my penis. That was uncomfortable and no pain medicine was administered for it. That felt very strange but only lasted a few moments. Then he proclaimed that we were done by saying he had captured and removed the kidney stone. The strange feeling that I had in my private area did not go away though. I waited a moment and then asked; are you going to take the tube out? Without hesitation, he said "No, I am going to leave it in for a few weeks, in case this happens again."

I was relieved that the stone was gone but I was not happy at all about what he just said. "A few weeks?" Are you kidding me? He was not kidding but he was serious. What was I to do? He was a medical professional and knew better than I. The other weird part of all that was, there was a string hanging out of the end of this tube that was in my penis. It was essentially a fishing pole that was inside of me.

The next few weeks were quite uncomfortable and I can say that I would have much rather urinated through a funnel again than deal with all of that. It gave me a burning sensation, every single time I had to go to the bathroom. On my check-up, which was about three weeks later, the doctor had the results of the first kidney stone back. It was a nine out of ten on the hardness scale. It was almost like bone, with a heavy calcium component to it.

On that day we talked about my diet and the changes that I was making and further changes that needed to be made. I had been a heavy soda drinker; my particular choice of soda had a large amount of sugar in it. My medical provider advised me that was one of the worst things I was consuming. It was his opinion that this was a leading culprit to my back-to-back kidney stone attacks.

During that time, I cut back drastically on hard liquor, cut soda out completely, and became a tea drinker. Sweet tea, iced tea, and bottled tea. Eventually, I quit smoking once again. I had quit cigarettes prior but resumed that addiction with the aforementioned legal troubles.

It is amazing to me how we do those things to our bodies and how we can recover from the damage if we heed the warning signs. God sometimes has to knock loudly on the doors of hearts to get our attention. That was the beginning of my awakening in both the physical and spiritual realms.

Chapter 14 Takeaway: Healthier Choices

I had asked for God's will to be done and He brought me home.
I needed to rest and repair the damage I had done with my poor choices.
How do you walk in and not against God's direction for your life?

Bible verses to reflect upon:
Psalms 119:105
John 15:7

Chapter 15

Moving on

The kidney stones experience happened that fall season shortly after moving back home. The holidays came and went and we entered into a new year. My sister and her husband decided they were going to move and they did not want me to come along on the journey. Her husband was granted custody of his child from his first marriage. The child was a teenage boy and I believe he was going through the trials of life that all teenagers go through. They wanted to be a family and honestly, they were having marriage issues that they were working out. It was time for me to move on.

I had very limited options at this time. My mother was living with her mother, and my second oldest sister and her husband had moved to Florida several years earlier. I do not recall how the initial conversations went but I am sure my oldest sister approached my dad about my coming back out to the house to live with him and my youngest sister.

That is what happened. My youngest sister graduated high school that year and decided to go to college. She decided to attend the same local college my mother had gone to because of a relationship she was in at the time. During that time, I helped out around the house as much as I could. We lived on a five-acre lot of land out in the country. There was much mowing that needed to be done even with our large pond in the backyard.

I continued with the party lifestyle but it was greatly toned down. I had had my fill of legal troubles and more recently my health concerns. Then one day my dad announced that he was selling the house and was going to move in with his new wife. He had been dating this woman for a while and she had her own place. They had taken a trip to another state and had eloped!

Another season of transition was about to begin for me. As I had few friends during this time. In high school, I had been accused of being a Satan worshiper because of the book that I read and the trouble I had with drugs, alcohol, and vandalism. My bad reputation preceded me most of the time. The few friends I had were either married with children or they too lived at home with a parent. What happened with an open door was out of necessity and an act of kindness from a casual friend.

His brother and my brother-in-law both owned land parcels side by side. His brother was building a house and my sister and her husband had not yet developed anything. They had purchased a home in town that they moved to when I went back out to live with my dad and youngest sister; they had this property as well. The man was kind enough to allow me to move in with him and his young son. He had an apartment and I was able to have a bedroom to myself and that was nice.

The bad part about all that was, no animals were allowed to live there. That is where the land my sister had, came into the picture. I had my faithful companion from college, he had made it from there to my sister's to my dad's and now he was going to be out in the woods by himself. It broke my heart and was not easy on either one of us. I had a large kennel and put a roof on it and tarps for shelter. He was out there for months, all summer long and into the fall. I went out there daily to spend time with him and take him for drives and go to different places.

This was my companion and I did not know how we were going to get back together in a warm safe place to call home before winter. There was an adjacent farmhouse that had a family with two teenage boys living there. I found out they had been shooting at my dog with a BB gun because I discovered my dog had a BB lodged in his ear and there were other signs as well. He had that BB in his ear until he passed away. In later veterinarian visits, they said it was fine and left it alone.

I never taught those boys a lesson although I wanted to; I also did not want any more trouble with the law. One day, I asked them about "people" shooting at my dog and they of course denied it and lied about it to me. Thankfully there was traffic back and forth at the property because of my brother-in-law's friend building his house there. This was one of the first times I had to let go and let God handle that situation.

During this time again, my relationship with my dad had not been on solid ground. We did talk and eventually, he had compassion for me and helped me to get a place to live that fall. God's hand had been upon my dog as I prayed daily for him. God answered my prayers about having a place to live with my dog.

Chapter 15 Takeaway: God's Provision

Multiple moves are stressful and difficult to cope with or handle. I had been praying to God daily for a home and His provision came through.
How do you pray when you have no clear vision?

Bible verses to reflect upon:
Psalms 33:20
James 1:6

Chapter 16

The Wicked Woman

My dad knew a single man who had been living in a small home in a local mobile home park. This man worked out a deal with my dad and he bought the mobile home outright. It was a small older single-wide home by a local ball field where the school played many of its baseball games. Since this was a park, even though the home was paid for in full, lot rent was due each month. I found out from the homeowner when rent was due and where the office was. I was not prepared for what was about to happen.

The first time I went and knocked on this person's door, an older woman opened the door. When I introduced myself as the new owner of the said mobile home, there was quite a lengthy exchange, most of it coming from her. She proceeded to tell me that she did not know the home had been sold to me and that I was not welcome there. I had my dog with me in my vehicle and she said that dogs of that size were not allowed in the park either. She also had a fully negative representation of who I was. This woman did not know me, as we had never met. However, my reputation in my small hometown had once again preceded me.

As she rejected my money and my presence, she told me that neither my dog nor I were welcome in her park and that I needed to leave. I had tears streaming down my face as she spewed her hatred of me back to me. Rejected, dejected, and insulted I left. Phone calls had to be made. First, my dad, and after talking to him then the man who sold him the trailer. Those conversations led to a lawyer conversation. I could not believe what was happening to me.

When I talked to a real estate lawyer, I was advised to open an escrow account and pay my full rent on time, each month. At his advice, I did so through the courthouse. There was a coming legal battle with the woman and her husband. This battle took almost a year to get resolved and there were many things about to unfold during this time; including an old friend coming back into my life to betray me one final time.

This time lasted from one fall season until the next fall season. Many things happened including multiple eviction notices, which I had to ignore. You cannot evict someone out of a house that they own, which had been paid for in full. She and her husband were trying to evict me out of their mobile home park. During this time, they even shut my water off. I was able to get it back on and had to pay my own utilities, so at least those were safe. I began to leave my dog at home for security reasons. He was a large German Shepherd and Great Dane mix and the landlords were afraid of him.

My so-called best friend from high school came back into my life. Before leaving for college, I know my then fiancé slept with him one night. I asked him about it and he denied it but said later after I was gone that he went out with her once. It was an insult to injury as he was also the same person involved with the infamous marijuana fight that led to my leg breaking as previously mentioned. He wanted marijuana and asked about where I was getting my supply. Red flags were appearing and we did not hang out during this time because I simply could not trust him for obvious reasons. This was back in the 1990s and wireless home phones were still relatively new but I had one.

Something strange happened a short time after he visited my trailer home. One night a police car was parked in the ball field parking lot and it was a revelation in the spirit to me, that they were scanning frequencies trying to listen in on my phone calls. Marijuana was illegal in all fifty states back then, but I still used it. With my landlords trying to evict me and a former friend's betrayal, I had to keep a close circle of friends.

In the spring of that year, I had asked God to show me something from my past. Who was I and where did I come from? I had a close friend in college who stayed connected with me even though he moved back to his home state and I mine. He had a deep knowledge of history and made me think about things I normally would not think of when we would talk.

What happened through some of these conversations was just that, me asking questions to God about those things. One night He showed me something. I had this intense dream of sword training with a cloaked figure. I could not see a face but this shadow figure was wearing a flowing robe that was grayish-black in color. There were maneuvers performed during this dream sequence that I had never done in my life. The dream was not violent; it was a sword-training dream. I shared this experience with my old hippy friend that I smoked marijuana with and his response was simply "what did you eat last night?"

You can speculate that the dream related to what was going on in my life. Physical battles with legal troubles in real estate and spiritual battles going on around me. It was something that was extremely vivid and stuck with me, even all of these years. As the fall approached, a court date was set and this was going to come to an end. Much like my old high school friend coming back into my life, I did not see the outcome that was about to unfold before me.

Chapter 16 Takeaway:
Trials and Tribulations

I had gone through much trouble and thought there was a place for me there.
I was persecuted and hated by someone who did not know me.
How do you rely on God when you face adversities in your life?

Bible verses to reflect upon:
Psalms 18:28-30
I Peter 3:14-16

Chapter 17

The Last Straw

I will say that one's reputation can be a hard thing to reconcile. When we finally went to court several things happened. The man that sold me the trailer had to testify, the landlords had to testify, and then I had to testify. You might as well have thrown it all out the window.

Here is what the court decided: the landlords, the plaintiffs were awarded all of the lot rent money. That was no surprise as I had expected that portion of the judgment. I was ordered to remove the mobile home from the park within ten days of the court-ordered ruling. My counterclaims against the landlord were dismissed, as was a cross-claim against the man who sold my dad the trailer. That was a shock but I should have known it was coming.

There was a visiting judge who had been assigned from the supreme court of the state. That happened because during a previous court appearance, the proceedings were not recorded and my then-lawyer did not represent me well. My old hippy friend was a friend to the lawyer and when I shared the details of what happened. He advised me, that the supreme court of the state holds lawyers accountable in those matters.

I filed a complaint against the lawyer and gave full details of what had happened at the previous trial and the supreme court of the state did question my former lawyer who was very angry with me and was no longer my lawyer. The court proceedings were questioned as well. I had stirred the hornet's nest and somehow thought that justice would be served in my favor. I had come to the wrong conclusion about the outcome and it was the final straw. The turn of those events is what made me decide to plan my permanent exit. My dad was furious with the landlords, as he knew them. He also knew the man who sold him the trailer. My dad made arrangements to have the trailer hauled out of the park with a local farmer using a large tractor.

My sister and her husband had purchased a second piece of land outside of the town limits. I was able to arrange for the trailer to be relocated there and chose to sell it. The property had no utilities of any kind at the time. I was now homeless as that wicked woman had won her battle in court and I was thoroughly dejected and disgusted with my hometown. I wanted to leave and never come back. My sister and her husband took me in once again. I think my whole family was shocked at the biased outcome of the court.

I felt worse than you can imagine and I developed a genuine hatred of the small backwoods town that I had called home. It was time to take action, how was I going to leave and where was I going to go? It's funny how sometimes things happen and you don't know why they do.

I had a friend that I would still party with, drinking alcohol and smoking marijuana. One day we decided to go to the city across the state line and while he was driving, a young man ran a traffic light and T-boned us incredibly hard.

He hit us so hard it lifted the vehicle we were in up off the ground. The impact was on the driver's side. We were drinking and driving as we had open beers in the vehicle. He was driving a nice sports car and had a carload of friends with him. That young man after it happened was laughing about it and I had to stop my friend from going over and starting a fight with him. My friend was furious and I was not happy either. The police and the paramedics came to the scene.

Somehow, my friend did not get into any trouble for an open beer. Mine had spilled on me and the paramedic smelled it on me and asked about us drinking. He was an old acquaintance from high school, as we had graduated together.

The accident was bad but could have been worse. God had spared us and as it happened, my friend and I had been talking about deja vu. I was sharing with him some of my vivid dream experiences that would later come true exactly as I had dreamed them. Sometimes it was weeks later other times it was months later.

After the accident, I went to go see a local chiropractor. In a strange turn of events, perhaps because of what I told the paramedics I began treatment with this new doctor. I was hurt on the day of the accident with what later turned out to be sideways whiplash. It may sound made up but it is not, it is similar to whiplash, which happens when you are hit in the rear of a vehicle and suffer a back injury with pain. It was estimated the driver of the other vehicle was traveling at least thirty-five mph. We were going just as fast, as we had the green light. That was quite an impact on the vehicle and us. The chiropractor wanted to treat me three times a week for a lengthy period of time, something like eight weeks, and then follow-up treatments after that.

It did not take long for the insurance company to come and make me a financial offer. I turned down that initial offer but in hindsight, I should have taken it. Instead, I listened to certain family members and hired an attorney. In the process of doing the treatments and attempting to sue, I lost my friendship with the man I was in the accident with. He was angry and jealous that I was having the attention of a doctor and now a lawyer and his vehicle had still not been repaired. That was in the fall season almost immediately after the trailer trial and God was working things in my favor to lead me to my own exodus.

Chapter 17 Takeaway: God Will Provide

The battle had come to an end. What felt like defeat was the beginning of my victory.
When you are faced with great difficulty, do you trust God?

Bible verses to reflect upon:
Psalms 138:7
Philippians 4:19

Chapter 18

A Second Chance

As the end of the year approached, I was required to appear before a medical doctor for a review of my disability claim. This had been in effect since the breaking of my leg back in my senior year of high school. The original surgeon decided to put two stainless steel screws in my leg back then as he thought it would help the bones fuse together and strengthen them. He was mistaken, and in fact, he had been dead wrong about that.

What happened was my leg rejected the screws and grew around them. The result was my leg became bowed at a thirty-five-degree angle and then the doctor who put the screws in my leg wanted to rebreak my leg. My dad at the time had high-quality insurance with his job and decided he would arrange for me to go to a world-renowned facility in our state. Once there, my new doctor decided to use what was called the Ilizarov method, which had been developed in Russia and had primarily been used for neck injuries.

That new doctor and the use of this apparatus saved my leg. How it worked was they drilled holes in my leg and inserted thin metal rods, in one side of the leg and out the other. These metal rods were attached to large metal rings that encased and protected my leg. There were dials and I had to make small millimeter adjustments each day. The device slowly bent my leg back to where it was originally intended to be. The other key part of this was, there had to be a gap for both bones, both the tibia and fibula to move. What they had to do was remove a section of bone to allow for movement. My foot and ankle were essentially suspended with the support of the lower ring.

It was working perfectly until one day I had extreme pain. This happened while I was trying to make the adjustments. An emergency visit to the facility resulted in them taking an x-ray and discovering that the critical gap to allow for movement had grown shut. They were going to have to operate, again. I can tell you that when I awoke in recovery I began to scream in pain.

The doctor and my mother stood at the front of the room and were talking about what; I had no idea at the time. Due to my screams of pain, they administered more and more pain medicine until the pain calmed down. What I later found out was they were talking about my illegal drug use because the doctor was shocked at how much pain medicine they had to administer.

I will say that was the worst pain I had ever experienced and why did it hurt so bad? Because of the lengthy surgery of putting the device on me, I believe it was around four hours to do so, they decided to break the bone with a hammer and chisel. You read that correctly, they beat my leg until it broke.

Years later when I had the kidney stone attacks that would be the second worse pain compared to that one. It sounds terrible but it was a success. It was a long process and through it all, I had remained on disability but now it was time to let that go. The doctor that I was currently seeing was a state-appointed one to review my disability and to see what I could do for employment.

Through the evaluation, we talked about what would I like to do? The state was willing to pay a certain amount for vocational or educational training to get me off of the state disability and insurance. That is where my second college came into focus. It just took a little paperwork and the next thing I knew, I was going to be headed to an audio college in the spring.

Through the time leading up to that joyful event in my life, God began to show me things in dreams. You see, I was at a major turning point in my life. I had been living on disability, smoking marijuana, and drinking alcohol. I had quit cigarettes for the second time in my life but still had those other two addictions.

The hard drugs came to an end too when I had my first bad experience with LSD. I was with my old hippy friend one night, and we were in the city across the state line and stopped in to see a friend of his. His friend had some powder cocaine and shared it with us. I was not a cocaine user as it was an expensive high and there was the paranoia that came with the high. That is where my LSD trip went bad. After mixing those two dangerous substances in my body, that was it. I was done and would have nothing more to do with hard drugs anymore. Through that process and a later angelic encounter, I realized through that nudge from God above that it was time to move on.

One day I was at my old hippy friend's house and we had smoked marijuana. It was a nice day outside and I believe this was in the late summer before the trailer verdict came down. I decided to go outside and get some fresh air. While I was sitting on his front steps I heard very distinctly "get in the car and leave." Now I was high on marijuana at the time, so I sat there. As I thought that was weird, what was that? Again, the voice came to me and was now angry. The voice said, "do I have to pull you by the ponytail and put you in the car myself?" At the time I had hair down to my waist and kept it pulled back most of the time. I got up and left but I did reason within myself, what would my friend think? I just got up and left without saying goodbye.

I do not know what the Lord kept me from that day, only after the LSD-cocaine incident; there was a heightened awareness of things going on with my friend. I am referring to the terrible night that I went through and I had noticed off in the distance a police presence. Later I would find out they were watching my friend due to his ties to the marijuana drug world. God led me away from that man, kept me from harm in the physical, and eventually I stopped smoking marijuana as well.

Chapter 18 Takeaway: Healing and Health

God had restored my health in my body and had sent a clear message that began restoring my mind.
Have you ever been chastened by the Lord?

Bible verses to reflect upon:
Isaiah 40:31
Revelation 3:19

Chapter 19

Dangerous Dreams

There were several events that I will share with you as God guides me. One night I had a dream that I was in a railroad yard. There was an elevated line on a long smooth hill and train traffic in the background. I was by myself out in the yard and it was evening time almost dark when two men approached me. The men were plain clothes detectives. They asked about my old hippy friend and they wanted to know where he was.

That was an ominous dream with very dark undertones. The dream was in color as all of mine are but it was almost black and white. It was dark and dimly lit. The men faded away and I heard a distinct voice again, say, "there is a train coming through and you don't want to be on it." God was showing me through my eyes in the physical and now in a dream in the spiritual that my friend was under surveillance and that I needed to get away and stay away from him, his home, and his associates.

I had another dream not too long after this, but it was an out-of-body experience. One night I went to sleep on my twin bed in the den of my sister's home. The den was located in the front of the home close to the front door. Just as I went to sleep, I woke up only I was in the spirit. This may sound weird but I was standing by myself at the side of my bed. I stood there for a moment wondering why I was out of my body. I floated over to my antique mirror that had been in the family for decades and wanted to see what I looked like. Again, this may sound very strange but I was outside of my body.

The first time this happened I was in jail years ago, then on LSD in college, and now in my sister's house. What was going on here? I want to point out, that much like my LSD out-of-body experience, I had not asked for the experience to happen, it just did. At that time, I was not doing drugs of any kind and it was a genuine experience just like the jail experience was. When I saw myself in the mirror, it was not what I was expecting and it was not a reflection of my flesh body. Almost immediately after looking into the mirror, there was a shift in the room and a dark presence entered. I knew something bad was about to unfold, so I stood there at my bedside screaming at myself to wake up.

There appeared two entities that looked like black vapor in appearance, they were about four feet tall and they had a ghost-like shape to them. They had no feet, their body shape came down to a point and they floated. They initially appeared to be a solid form but then one spoke and quickly grabbed me. All of a sudden there was a set of arms and the entity had me in a tight grip. The other one just stood there, like it was there as backup or support.

Friends, this is not an easy thing to write and you may be thinking this sounds odd but what I am about to say may shake your religious foundations or ideology. When the spirit grabbed me and had me in a body grip to where I could not move. It spoke to me and said, "Do you want to go to hell, Shane?" What happened next was perhaps the most frightening thing I had ever seen. The floor below me opened up, the earth below the floor opened up and I saw an orange fiery glow coming up from the depths of the earth. I said "No!" and broke free from that spirit. As quickly as all of this happened, it ended. I woke up immediately after and was back in my body. The spirits were gone and the floor was closed up.

That was a major turning point for me. I knew God was calling me to something greater than myself and I was attempting to get on the road that was being laid before me. I believe that hell is very real and I saw a tiny glimpse of it in my bedroom that night. Why? I had been living in the "gray" area of life. I had been thinking there is black and white as in right and wrong but there is a big gray area in between. It's like riding the fence. God was calling on me to make a choice. I had been on the fence long enough, was I going to live for God or the devil?

One night in January, my sister came in and woke me up because my dog was making all kinds of noise outside. My brother-in-law had allowed me to come and stay with them but had put his foot down about my dog. The dog had to stay outside with their dog and that was all there was to it. They each had a doghouse and straw to keep warm. I had given my dog a blanket but there was something else going on in the air that night.

I went outside to see what was going on with my dog and he was so excited to see me. He was extremely wound up. It was very cold and I knew how my sister's husband felt but it was too cold for me to stay out there, so I brought my dog inside. I took a blanket and put it at the bottom of my bedroom door to try to deaden any sound that my dog might make. Because my room was next to the front door, it had been quite easy to get him into the house. I went back to bed and my dog slept with me. A twin-size bed for a full-size German Shepherd and me, we went to sleep.

I then found myself in a large cavernous cave and there were images of things including a Bible and an NFL player whom I looked up to, who served God as a minister. As we walked further along, my dog was with me and on a leash and we entered another area. There was a magnificent creature that God had made; it was a large red dragon with thin yellow stripes. When I saw it, I simply said, "awesome." It did not interact with us but was there just as the images of the things of God had been in the other room or chamber.

Finally, there was a third area to this cave-like structure we were in. Once we were in that final chamber, there was a decision placed before me that I had to make. I find it interesting that my dog had thrown a fit and my sister woke up to go calm him down. Now, here he was with me in this God-given experience, as I had to make my choice. I made my decision and then woke up.

This was a deeply personal experience with God, no I did not see God nor did I talk to Him in this process. It was a final test and I had to choose but He allowed my dog to be with me. My faithful companion knew there were angels around and knew something was going to happen that night. It is of no strange coincidence that he was with me. For you see, the large German Shepherd-Great Dane mix was my guardian in this life, his name was Cooper.

Chapter 19 Takeaway: Spiritual Decisions

God had called me to make a choice and I had to choose right then, was I going to serve God or the devil? I chose God!
Is God knocking on the door of your heart?

Bible verses to reflect upon:
Joel 2:28
Revelation 3:20

Chapter 20

My Exodus

Things began to align after the dream experience from God. My second college was upon me and I had to be ready for that. The college was located about two and half hours from where I was living. No pets were allowed there and my brother-in-law had informed me that my dog had to go when I left for college. He was being harsh with me and I thought at the time it was all directed at me. However, looking back, he had much trouble in his life. He had purchased two different plots of land, this large house, and his marriage had ended.

With the stress of that situation, I did the only thing I could and ask my mother if my dog could come to stay with her and grandma. My grandma was against the idea but softened to it after I let her know I could set up my large dog kennel for him and he could stay outside. I left my things at my sister and brother-in-law's house for the duration of my college stay. This was for about three months. The college was kind of a concentrated associate's degree program. We had class, working labs and were in class eight to ten hours a day, five days a week.

During this time, I shared a private cabin with another young man. It was a small one-bedroom house. We got along well and both of us drank alcohol at times. I was committed to not drinking through the week and slipped up once or twice and my roommate called me on it and helped keep me in check. We had the weekends off, which meant we could travel back home if we desired to do so. I went home every weekend except for one.

My dog became lethargic and seemed depressed, so I came home after that every weekend. On that one weekend, I had chosen to stay in the college town to drink with friends. What happened again was a turning point for me. I talked to my mother mid-week and she informed me that my dog was not well. When classes concluded on that Friday, I then drove home. My dog had grown on my grandmother and she allowed him to come into the house. Perhaps because of my absence that week, he was missing me. I knew he was not eating right and was sleeping most of the time from what my mother had told me.

This turned out to be a blessing as Cooper was used to being an inside-outside dog and it was springtime. Temperatures got pretty cold at night. He was glad to see me and he revived in my presence. I don't know who coined the phrase that a dog is man's best friend but it is true. He loved to go for rides and I recall asking him if he wanted to go for a ride. He sprang up and we went for a drive.

After this when I would come home on the weekend's I would check in with my brother-in-law as I had my belongings in his house and my sister had moved out and had herself a little apartment. Even with the stress between my brother-in-law and me, he allowed my things to stay there until I was done with college and was going to be moving on.

I had stopped smoking marijuana and had almost stopped drinking at this point. One of the first weekends that I came home from college, I stopped by my old hippy friend's house and smoked a single marijuana joint with him. I had been reluctant to do so and immediately regretted it. I left and when I got to my grandmother's house my mom was there and asked me what was wrong. I told her what had happened and she assured me that everything was going to be ok. She talked to me about God and His plans for me, she encouraged me to keep pressing on.

That was the last time that I ever smoked marijuana and I decided to leave that addiction in my home state when I left. Since I no longer was into partying that added an additional layer of tension between my brother-in-law and me. I would end up staying the night at my grandmother's house and sleeping on her couch in the living room.

Chapter 20 Takeaway: Praying the Way

It had been a long road but God was opening doors and closing them before me.
Prayer changes things and helps guide your steps. Do you pray daily?

Bible verses to reflect upon:
Isaiah 55:11
Revelation 3:7

Chapter 21

Spiritual Visitors

While staying at my grandmother's house I experienced several spiritual experiences from God. She was the most God-fearing woman that I knew and there were angels in and around her house. My mother lived there for a season as she was transitioning in her life as well. Her father had passed away when I had just left for my first college in 1993. Grandma had kept his favorite chair but had given away his clothes.

He was a big man, six foot two inches and in his later years he had put on much weight. Sadly, he had to be put in a home because it was too much for my grandmother to try to take care of him. My whole life he had been a quiet man, who spoke few words most of the time. He would engage in conversation if you asked him something and was genuinely a truly kind man. He and my grandmother lived through the great depression of the 1930s. They were a young married couple during that time. They worked hard their whole lives, they had a farm and she was a nurse at the local hospital for many years. Later, they leased the farm out and moved to the town where I was now sleeping on their couch on the weekends.

One night I went to sleep and had a visit from my grandfather. He was sitting in my grandmother's chair. Please understand, I did not ask for the experience nor I did not pray for it to happen. This was a God-given appointment that happened. He appeared to be in his early 30s and he had a golden glow about him. Not white but golden. He spoke to me about Heaven and that there was great hope in me. I sat there and listened, I don't recall saying anything. I was astounded that this was happening. I had wanted to be a successful musician with a band for as long as I could remember. Going all the way back to the age of nine. My grandfather did not give me any specifics or steps to take. It was a positive message of hope and faith.

I now knew hell and heaven were both real places and that with no doubt there is an afterlife. I shared the experience with my mother but not my grandmother at the time. I felt it was not necessary or that it might upset her in some way. It was only the beginning of revelations for me. There was a musician who had died in the 1980s that I related to and felt connected to. He had a strong presence in his band and left an impact on many people in the world. One night I had a vision of being in a large arena and there was a band performing. The style of music that was performed was of the heavy metal genre. At the concerts of these artists, people can get worked up into a frenzy of energy due to the music and lyrics. There are outbreaks of what are called mosh pits, I cannot say exactly where that term came from but that is what it is called.

In this vision, that was what was going on in small outbreaks on the arena floor. In the air above all of that scene, a large Bible opened up and God spoke to me. What He said was profound; He spoke to me about that particular musician and his writing. You see the young man had written several deeply spiritual and Biblical themed songs in the heavy metal genre before he died. God gave me a command and He used a word I had never heard before, "mattle." It was "Go forth and mattle." The other part of that particular God experience was that not only were the words spoken but they also appeared written. Just as the Bible was open with a red ribbon marker as God spoke. I interrupted the word mattle as to what I had seen in this vision. Stirring up people with the truth of God's Word through music.

When I asked my mother about it, she had no clue and years later when looking for that word, it could not be found. The music that I was listening to and whom God was speaking about during this experience, he had written music that made people think. Talking about deeper things in life and "waking" people up back in the '80s. I knew what I needed to do as I began to prepare for a new location.

That experience was astonishing to me. First, my grandfather spoke to me about a great hope in me, and then God spoke to me in the other experience. I want to emphasize that both of those experiences were neither asked for nor prayed for. They just happened. I did not see God in the vision but I know it was God who spoke to me and gave me a command. I was not sure how I was going to accomplish it but that was only the beginning.

Chapter 21 Takeaway: Spiritual Direction

I had been seeking God and His direction.
God chose to show me His direction in my dreams.
How do you hear from the Lord and obey?

Bible verses to reflect upon:
Jeremiah 7:23
Hebrews 1:14

Chapter 22

The Enemy

After these miraculous visions from God, something strange happened one night in our one-bedroom house at the college. It occurred during the week as we had been attending classes. My roommate and I each had our own twin beds and we had gone to sleep for the night. I woke up in the middle of the night and could not move. I could only look around the room with my eyes. Sound familiar?

Just as I awoke and could not move, across the room there appeared a blinding white light. The light changed into a figure, and what was standing before me appeared to be Jesus Christ. He was clothed in a white robe, had sandals on his feet, and was of an average height, human in appearance with a dark beard and he had shoulder-length hair. When that happened, I looked over at my roommate, he was sound asleep and unaware. What happened bothered me for years.

If this was the Lord Jesus Christ, why could I not move? The other perhaps most important part of the encounter was he said nothing to me. He simply stood in the corner of the room across from our beds, glowing brightly. During the experience, I did have the thought of "why can't I move" and that this had previously happened when I had three demons visit me all at once. I was in a state of sleep paralysis and could only look around the room with my eyes. You might think that it was a glorious event but it was not. It troubled me for years and made me question many things. I do not recall going back to sleep but I did and when I awoke everything was back to normal. I did not share the experience with anyone because I was perplexed by it.

A few weeks later, I had finished college and prepared myself to relocate to Florida where one of my sisters lived. During that time, my friend from the first college, who had a deep knowledge of history and was a confidant, wanted me to relocate to his home state. His state, however, was a cold-weather state as well and I simply had had enough of winter. I had spent my entire life up until that point in the Midwest and when winter came in each year by around Thanksgiving time, it did not leave until late April. I was determined to head to the sunshine state.

Now back to my encounter with what appeared to be the Lord Jesus Christ. I must fast forward here to give you the answer that I received. Many years later I was in a Pentecostal church and my pastor was preaching about Satan being able to transform himself into an angel of light. As soon as the words had left his mouth, the Lord immediately brought the memory back to my attention. Satan had come to visit me that night when I was in my bed asleep and he appeared to me as Jesus.

Why did he do that? Because at the time God had shown me great wonders and visions in my sleep life and I was in a period of great transition. God had placed a calling on my life and Satan was trying to derail me from fulfilling that calling.

Chapter 22 Takeaway: Don't be Deceived

During this time I was not praying enough.
You must put on the whole armor of God.
Do you pray throughout the day and rely on God?

Bible verses to reflect upon:
Psalms 55:22
2 Corinthians 11:14

Chapter 23

Headed South

The day had come for me to fly south to the sunshine state and to find my new home and my new life. I remember flying into Tampa and my brother-in-law picking me up. It was a profound moment for me, as I deeply desired to put the Midwest behind me. I stayed with him and my sister for what was going to be two weeks originally but turned into thirty days.

I had great difficulty finding work in my area of study. I had gone through audio recording engineering; more simply put I was now skilled to work in a recording studio. The problem with that market back then in the late 1990s was almost everyone I talked to offered me an unpaid internship. I could have gotten work my first week if I wanted to work for free. This was not going to work for me as I was going to have bills to pay.

I continued looking; I went to or called anything and everything that had anything to do with audio mixing, recording, or editing. Nothing happened until one day a man agreed to hire me to do audio recording and mixing for message on-hold calls. You know, "your call is important to us." I explained to him that I had to go back to the Midwest, pack up a truck and then make the move to Florida. He agreed and I was to begin work in two weeks.

Now, with the job settled the other question for me was; where was I going to live? My sister and her husband had been in Florida for about eight years at that point and were well established with friends and connections. One of her friends had a friend that was looking for a housemate. She was single and looking for someone to rent a room from her and share common spaces with. We talked and then I had to have an in-person meeting with her. It went well and I told her about my dog, which at that point I had him for four years. She and I agreed on terms and I was then ready to head back home to pack a truck and travel back to Florida with my dog.

Remember how my dog had missed me when I was gone for more than a week? I was gone for a month and he did just fine during that time. I believe he knew I was finding us a home and would be back to get him. Perhaps the angels at my grandmother's house gave him peace during this time. All sounded good, right?

I went back home and it took about a week to get everything together. I had to arrange for a moving truck and car carrier. Then I had to get my belongings out of my brother-in-law's house. Lastly, I had to disassemble the dog kennel and pack it up. My mother's brother helped me with that task, it was early June and it was a warm sunny day. Funny, how we can remember the weather of an important day. I also remember putting my dog in the front seat of that moving truck and he was so happy. He knew we were going on a new adventure and he was just as excited as he could be. We were saying goodbye to the Midwest.

Chapter 23 Takeaway: Where There's a will

I had been planning the move for months and God had opened two key doors for me.
How do you know you are seeking His will for your life?

Bible verses to reflect upon:
Proverbs 8:17
Romans 13:14

Chapter 24

A Mistake?

The journey was long and it took a couple of days. It was just about one thousand one hundred miles. I drove many hours and we got to my sister's late the following evening. We had taken the I-75 interstate that allowed us to travel many miles in a day.

I had to tie my dog outside to a tree that first night because my sister had a cat and that is what had to happen for us to stay the night. The next morning, I wanted to go to our new place and tried to connect with the woman we were going to be living with. It was the age before everyone had a cell phone. I went to her house and she was not there. I called and she did not answer. I left multiple voice messages and she did not return my call to my sister's house. Finally, my sister got a hold of the woman's mutual friend and she, in turn, called her. At last, the woman called me and informed me that she had changed her mind.

Are you kidding me? My dog and I had just moved one thousand one hundred miles and she changed her mind. I was shocked and did not know what to do. My sister's mutual friend had a small house called a mother-in-law's quarters that was available on her property. She was willing to rent it to me. It was a small one-bedroom apartment house with a shared utility room. It was perfect for Cooper and me. We were glad to have it and it worked out better than the original plan.

After getting moved in and having a home phone number installed and activated. It was now time to follow up with the employer who had promised me a job. I called and left messages for the man, who had said he would put me to work when I got back to the Tampa area. He was always unavailable and never returned my call. One day, I had had enough and went downtown in person to their location. The man reluctantly came and spoke with me for a moment. He informed me that he had hired someone else. He simply did not believe me when I told him I was coming back. Why had the man lied to me and promised me a job? I was angry but did not lose my temper, as there was no job and I left. I called my sister to let her know what had happened and she said she would see if she could help me out with finding work.

I had received a settlement from the accident where I had been a passenger with my friend back in the Midwest. That was due to the sideways whiplash diagnosis and treatment plan that I had undergone. In hindsight, I would have been better off accepting their initial offer when I started my treatment. However, there had been enough money to pay the doctor's bills and to get myself moved to Florida. It was now time to get to work and start making some money. At that point, between the woman rejecting my dog and me from living in her home and the man flat out lying to me about having a job, I did ask the question: Did I make a mistake moving to Florida?

My sister was able to come through for me once again, first with the little house through her friend and now a job. It was through another friend of hers who was an office manager. She was willing to give me a job performing data entry at a pre-employment screening agency. My job was to verify people's applications for various companies that we were contracted with. It included making phone calls to colleges and universities, employers' past and present, and personal references. It was interesting work and I was thankful for the job. I did such a good job that when I received my first paycheck, I was surprised that they were paying me fifty cents more per hour than what I had been hired for. What a blessing that was!

It seemed like things were coming together after all. My sister had helped me out with finding a place to live and a job. I was doing just fine for the moment until an old acquaintance appeared in my life.

Chapter 24 Takeaway:
There's a way

People will do the opposite of what they say. God will never leave you or forsake you.
Do you believe that you receive when you ask God according to His will?

Bible verses to reflect upon:
Psalms 37:5
Mark 11:24

Chapter 25

The Bar

My oldest sister back in the Midwest gave my phone number to someone who was an acquaintance of mine back in high school. He was the older brother of a classmate of mine. This connection was casual, as my friendship with his younger brother was and I barely knew the man, I simply knew of him. He was in Florida on business, working in the next town over, and wanted to meet up with me for a drink.

He proceeded to tell me about a large bar, a nightclub that he went to, and said I would like it. The town was about thirty minutes away and I agreed to meet him on a Friday night after work. My current job was an office job with Monday through Friday hours. We met and I was shocked. Someone had converted an old grocery store into a bar. It was not just a bar, but there were four bars within one building. The place was packed and there were hundreds of people there. It was a themed nightclub, with country and western music in the front two bars and rock-n-roll in the back with an additional two bars. The funny thing was there was techno, hip-hop, dance music in the back; not rock-n-roll. I spent the following few weekends at the bar, as I had no real friends in Tampa and I developed friendships at the nightclub.

The man who introduced me to this club, a short while later betrayed my trust, and as quickly as our friendship developed it dissolved just as quickly. The seeds had been planted though in the large party atmosphere. I found myself spending my Friday and or Saturday nights there. Drinking and then driving from the bar back to my home in the Tampa area. I used to take back roads in addition to the interstate to where the bar was located.

I became a weekend regular and eventually started to work the weekends there as a barback. Simply explained that is a position where I would stock the bar with all the supplies. That would include alcohol, cups, ice, straws, and garnishments. Throughout the night I would restock the beer tubs, those were large metal farm tubs meant for holding drinking water for livestock and they were located behind the bar.

The owners had hired attractive women who sold beer in bikinis. These young ladies were on elevated platforms and would usually sell a lot of beer. I was always assigned two of those stations in addition to the back two bars. It was a fast-paced work environment as hundreds of people would come through the doors each night. I held on to my office job for as long as I could but eventually, it caught up with me. I had to be at work at a certain time on Friday night but of course, Saturday was not a problem as I was off from my other job.

One particular Friday, the office manager said something to me about my priorities not being straight and said I needed to choose between the bar and the office. A short time later, after talking to the bar manager and obtaining full-time employment, I quit my job at the office. The bar manager had been trying to get me to come work full time for a month or so as he was impressed with my speed and work ethic. It was an easy choice for me at the time, as I enjoyed my time at the bar, first as a customer, then as an employee. There was trouble on the horizon though.

I started dating a waitress to whom I was attracted. There was a slight problem though; she was engaged to another man. Our relationship was short-lived as for whatever reasons she had; she did choose to have a sexual relationship with me. She kept it from her fiancé and then eventually broke it off with him. She also quickly moved on to another man who worked at the bar. She broke off her engagement and ended our short-lived relationship.

It should have come as no surprise to me, considering her lack of character but it did. I was no saint in the matter either and the damage had been done. Her now ex-fiancé hated me and it grew with each weekend, as he would come in and watch me. Looking back at this, he was stalking me.

In the midst of all of it, God spoke to me the date of April 24th. He started speaking it to me many weeks in advance of the day. The thought that I had or was given was that her ex-fiancé was going to come to the bar with a handgun and kill me.

My old friend from college and I were talking about spiritual things at that time. I shared with him the date and he knew of my now previous relationship with the waitress. He advised me to come to see him and spend a week or two in his state. I arranged to take some time off and was originally going to miss just one week of work.

The plan was to leave on Monday and return the following week. I would have had about ten days for travel and visiting. My friend had developed a relationship with a woman who had two young children from her previous marriage. As it had been decided, I packed up my car and took my dog for a road trip that would take me a long way from the bar and any possible danger that was lurking about. God was removing me from a dangerous position and I was looking forward to seeing my old college friend.

Chapter 25 Takeaway: Driven by the Flesh

I was completely driven by the flesh in a wrong relationship with a woman.
God can direct your path even when you have made a terrible decision.
How do you keep your flesh from leading you astray?

Bible verses to reflect upon:
Psalms 119:11
1 Corinthians 10:12-13

Chapter 26

West Virginia

We were all set and headed north. I chose the most direct route to travel up the I-95 interstate. It went through several states, as the trip was about one thousand miles. We stopped along the way and continued the next day.

The strangest thing happened around Frederick, Maryland as we were approaching my friend's home. We were headed up a hill and my car just died, I mean it lost all power and would not go any further. We had come over nine hundred miles and my car died. Somehow I was able to call my friend and give him our location by mile marker. He came and towed me to his place and we were able to get the car looked at. It was beyond repair, we were able to mend it a little while later but I would have to acquire another vehicle for the return trip home. I do not recall exactly what happened except for it was a problem related to compression and an exhaust manifold problem. The car would barely move forward in town on flat roads.

My friend had made arrangements for my dog and me to stay at his girlfriend's house. He was staying there as well but still had belongings at his mother's house across town. Things were fine until my dog became protective of the couch we were sleeping on. His girlfriend was worried he was going to snap at one of her kids. From that point on, if I left the house my dog either came with me or was put outside. I understood her concerns and it was never a problem.

My friend and I would go out and drink at a local strip club that he liked and he showed me all around the backcountry roads and old homesteads. It was an interesting area with much history. I now understood why he loved history as much as he did.

One evening, we were out driving as the sun was going down. There was a small mountain in front of us or perhaps a very large hillside and forested area, covered with trees. I was looking straight ahead and my friend was driving, what I saw I could hardly believe that I was seeing. Black shadow spirits were flying to and fro from one side of the area to the other. The highway went right through the hillside. I pointed the spirits out to my friend and his response was "I know, that happens all the time." He had seen the spirits before and thought nothing of it. They were all black and varied a little in size but they were there and they were flying about. At this point in our lives, neither of us was doing drugs anymore. We had not drunk any alcohol at this point either. Those were real spirits in real-time and it was right in front of us. My friend had the spiritual gift of sight as well.

We had some good times throughout my time there and it was decided that I could buy a vehicle at an auction that was held monthly. I had just missed the one for that month. I was in communication with my manager and told him of the situation. He liked me, my work ethic and informed me that my job would be there when I returned.

I wound up spending a month at my friend's place. I had saved a lot of money before the trip and had brought most of my belongings with me in the trunk of my car. I honestly did not know what was going to happen once I got up there or if I would go back to Florida to live. I was able to purchase a vehicle and sell my old one for almost nothing as it barely made it to the driveline at the auction house. Since there had been several weeks leading up to it, my friend and I had spent much time together talking.

We were both audio engineers and guitar players and talked about opening a studio and playing music together. My friend wanted me to stay but I had to go back to Florida for the rest of my belongings. I had decided, that it would take about a month because I needed to work, save up more money and then move to his state.

God had not previously given me an answer on how long I was to be in West Virginia. I had planned on being gone for a total of about ten days. However, since there was great tension between the man at the bar and myself, God kept me away not for one week but one month. I believe that was to allow time for the man to cool off and for me to rekindle the bond with my old college friend.

As I left West Virginia, the last image I saw of my friend was of him looking rather sad that I was leaving in my rearview mirror, as he stood there with his girlfriend. I did feel the desire to return to Florida but I was unaware of what was ahead for me.

Chapter 26 Takeaway: Old friends

Sometimes we can be tempted to relive our past when we reunite with old friends. God knows all things including when it is time to leave or time to move on.
Do you trust God with all things past, present, and future?

Bible verses to reflect upon:
Psalms 32:8
Hebrews 11:1

Chapter 27

Returning to Florida

We traveled back to Florida, by this time my dog Cooper had become a regular traveler and was just happy to be with me. I settled back into my life as a barback and started to save up money again to make the move to West Virginia. I had kept the plan to myself except I confided in my sister that I felt close to my friend like he was a brother and wanted to move.

Sometimes we blame God for things that we do to ourselves. Do you recall me mentioning drinking and driving? Well, that finally caught up with me after being back in Florida just a few weeks.

On the night in question, I got so drunk that I passed out in the parking lot with my vehicle running. One of my co- workers knocked on the window to wake me up and asked if I was all right. I nodded my head yes and proceeded to pull myself together or at least I thought I had. Now for some reason, I decided to take the interstate home instead of the back roads. I should not have been driving either way as I was well past the legal limit.

The state trooper that pulled me over was a rather nice man and put up with me as I later saw the dashboard camera footage. I was a happy drunk and non-threatening but boy I could not stand still or walk a straight line. Off to jail, I went. He took me to the county jail and my vehicle was impounded. Looking back at the series of events leading to my arrest, I thank God that I did not hurt anyone or cause any accidents.

My sister bailed me out of jail and a short while later my dad showed up with her. He was an over-the-road truck driver and was in town, which was something he did while driving, he would visit my sister and her family for a day. They took me to get the vehicle out of the impound yard and I had to apply for a hardship license to drive to and from work.

There were many things that I would have to do to get my license back but the first thing was to hire an attorney at my sister's insistence. As mentioned about the footage, after seeing it in the lawyer's office, we had no chance of arguing anything. I was going to be guilty as charged.

In an instant, the plans of moving to West Virginia were gone and I now had an uphill legal battle that was going to cost thousands of dollars before it was over. One of the hardest phone calls I had to make was to my old college friend to give him the news of what happened. He was disappointed but understood what happened as we both still liked to drink.

Many things happened but I will just summarize by saying I had to go to a psychologist to take a test, which determined how many therapy sessions I would have to attend. The answer was twelve and that portion of my sentence was costly in the financial sense. Through it though, I had to take a hard look at myself and what I was doing to my health. I was twenty-seven years old and had been drinking my life away. As if that was not enough to show me I had a problem, there was one more trial I would have to go through and it almost cost me my life.

Chapter 27 Takeaway: Last Call

I was clearly not in control of my drinking and had let my flesh rule my actions.
Have you ever said "I'm good" in reference to an addiction like drinking and thought you were in control?
How do we stay focused on God and not the flesh?

Bible verses to reflect upon:
Psalms 119:15-16
Romans 12:1-2

Chapter 28

The Trip Home

My youngest sister was going to be getting married in July 1999. My oldest sister had gotten married to her second husband in May of that same year. I could not afford to take two trips back to the Midwest, so I went home to my younger sister's wedding. I was a groomsman in their wedding party.

I had only been gone from the area just over a year and at the rehearsal, at the church, someone was disrespectful to me and it hurt. We were in the kitchen area of the church and the younger brother of a casual friend of mine brought up my past in front of everyone. He asked a very ignorant and insensitive question; was I still a Satan worshiper? I was shocked by his question, as were the people around me as well.

You see, once again my reputation preceded me. I was never a worshiper of the devil. I had made the mistake of reaching out into the darkness when I had been bullied in high school. Then shortly after that, I got into legal trouble with vandalism and the stigma stuck with me. That young man was a prime example of the sheer ignorance of some of the people in the town where I had been raised. I replied to his question with a quick "no, I never was." He quickly realized that he had offended me and perhaps all of the people in the room by his callous question and apologized to me.

The wedding was on a Saturday afternoon, followed by a reception in the next town over where my sister was going to college. I had been drinking a certain cognac liquor in Florida with my bartender friend who was training me to bartend at the time. I had previously enjoyed it and decided to buy a bottle. I went around the reception hall drinking shots with old friends. Most of them had never heard of that alcohol. There was draft beer available courtesy of my dad, who had paid for the reception.

It was his youngest daughter's wedding and the last daughter to be married. It was a nice reception and I had a good time until I sat down by my mother and she said what only a mother could say. "You don't look so good, Shane." I was drunk but I do recall being rude to my mother and using some foul language. She brushed it off, as there were many people there.

My mom and dad had been divorced for seven years at this point and my dad had married his second wife. He and my mother were tolerable of each other when together. My mom lived across the state line and had rented a hotel room with two beds so I could stay with her. I recall going back to the hotel with her and getting into my bed. Before doing so though, I looked into the mirror and saw that I was extremely red on the face and neck. I remember her asking me if I was all right and I said something to the effect of yes; I just need to sleep it off.

I found out later, that she left the room and had gone back to the reception. Drinking hard liquor straight, one shot after another had put me down rather early it seemed. What happened next was a near-death experience for me.

While I was asleep I was in an intense dream. I was in a large old hotel with many rooms and doors. There were beings there; not just humans but also people with long tails and some that were just creepy looking. One, in particular, was chasing me through the hallways and used what felt like an electric buzzer on the lowest point of my back. Located right in the center of the low back just above my buttocks. It was a real pain and strong shock, like being electrocuted in that area. The entity hit me with that shock many times, as I ran through the hallway trying to get away from him.

I finally found an open door and went through it. I was now in a large lobby area with a long bar, the room was well lit in traditional lighting with fixtures hanging above the bar. There were many barstools as I walked from the left side of the room, where the door was. I come around to the front of the bar, and my friend from the nightclub was there at the bar. He was a big countryman with a beard and long wavy hair. He was a bouncer at the club and here he was, dressed, as he would be at the club when on duty. I felt safe when he was around.

I immediately went up beside him and started telling him about what had been happening to me. He asked me where was this happening? I pointed over towards a second door, on my right-hand side and said back there. He was leaning slightly on the bar and then walked towards the door. He had a cowboy-style hat with him that was sitting on the bar. He would often wear this hat at the nightclub.

I stood there waiting for his return. During that time no one spoke to me and it did not seem like my friend was gone for very long. When he returned, he came back out through the same door he went in and said to me that "It's taken care of." I wanted to see what had happened and as I started to walk towards the same door that he came out of, he stopped me by grabbing my arm. He looked at me and said, "You don't want to go in there." I sat down on a barstool beside him and then woke up.

I was back in the hotel room, in bed. I looked over and my mother was asleep in the other bed. It was early morning. Friends it had been so real. It was a frightening experience that I could not wake up from while it was happening. I was perplexed by what had happened and when I got back to Florida, I reached out to my old college friend to seek his insight into what had happened.

After giving him all the details without hesitation he said God showed up. I then asked him how and why? He explained to me that God showed up in a form that I could understand and trust. My large friend was a tough man but was also a kind-hearted man. When I asked about the part of, "You don't want to go in there" reference, his explanation was simple enough. He said that God had destroyed those demonic spirits that were trying to kill me while I was fighting for my life with alcohol poisoning.

You see it was not my time to go. There was much work to be done and God intervened in that deadly situation. I could have and most probably would have died that night and would have been lost. I had been on my spiritual walk with God in my life as I prayed about things, but was not fully surrendered to Him at that point.

I decided I was going to quit drinking after all of that. I began to talk to God about quitting the addiction and turning my life around. God began a work in me that very moment.

Chapter 28 Takeaway: When Enough is Enough

My near-death experience with alcohol poisoning was the last straw.
Some people don't get the chance to quit and die in their addiction.
How do you keep your eyes and focus on God each day?

Bible verses to reflect upon:
Joshua 22:5
2 Peter 3:9

Chapter 29

A New Scene

The following spring my friend and his girlfriend came down to stay with me for a short while. They wanted to see me and check out Florida. It had been almost two years that I was living in the place that my sister's friend owned. My landlord, who was pregnant at that time, was in a relationship with another woman and had gone through artificial insemination to have a child. She had hidden the pregnancy for six months and could not hide it any longer.

I understand the stress she had in her life with the choices she had made. However, my friends coming and staying did not sit well with her. She was quite upset about it and they ended up going and staying at a local hotel after just a short time with me. My friend's girlfriend had recently become a stripper and that bothered my landlord. It is a profession that many look down upon with just cause. That exchange did not sit well with me at the time and I made plans to rent a house in the next town over with a co-worker there. I felt it was best to move out with all the drama going on in my landlord's life and move on.

I had also begun dating a woman from the bar and was spending a lot of time with her. My coworker and I had kind of an expensive place at the time and while we were both grown men, something strange happened there too. My roommate became jealous of the fact that I was not home much. My dog Cooper was there with him and his dog. Eventually, things boiled over and we went our separate ways. It was strange how it happened and I wound up putting most of my stuff in storage and moving in with my girlfriend.

That was not a good move and things quickly unraveled between us. My friend and his girlfriend along with her two children also lived in the same building. It was a large old house that someone had converted into a quadplex.

During my relationship with her, God showed me things in dreams that were quite real and what appeared to be from past events. Those situations that I was in, in the dreams, I had no memory of them happening. Some of these things were symbolic and related to my current girlfriend. I had many trials that I went through in the spirit. Many times I felt like I was in a season of training and most times those things were not pleasant. I would wake up in a sweat or be startled and as she was with me in bed, she would ask what was wrong or what had happened.

At one point she cared about me briefly and prayed her way of praying to stop my dreams and visions. When I spoke to her the next morning, she explained she had a terrible night of white walls going up before her and not being able to get through. When I shared the story with my friend, he was quick to point out she tried to interfere with God. Those dreams, visions, and spiritual trials that I had to go through were from Him and that is why she was running into giant white walls in her dream. It made sense to me as he explained it. After that happened, one of the last visions I had while I was in her bed, in her house was of me in deep water. I was underwater swimming around four giant spider webs. They were massive webs and there were no spiders in them. When I woke up, I had the revelation that those were the webs of lies that were in my girlfriend's life at the time.

I had Cooper with me at the time and she used the excuse of no large pets were allowed. She hinted that I should look at getting a place of my own. Funny, how things changed that quickly. I had a place of my own and gave that up to move in with her.

She had a teenage son living with her and that made things difficult as well. To no fault of his own, it turned out his mother went from boyfriend to boyfriend and many of them had lived with them previously. Things changed for the worse as she became friends with my friend's girlfriend and decided that she too would become a stripper. That was the quick downward spiral and end of our relationship. Strippers as I now knew from first-hand experience were driven by money and were users of men. Men were guilty of objectifying women and breathing life into that profession.

Just like that, I had to find somewhere else to live. A customer from the bar offered me a room to rent. He would not allow my dog to stay in his house, so I had to set up his doghouse and also had a tie out for him in the backyard. That too was short-lived as my friend had OCD, obsessive-compulsive disorder. I was unaware of that problem until one day he came home from work and I happened to be home at the time. I had left a single glass in the sink. He walked over to the sink to wash his hands, saw the glass, picked it up, and smashed it in the sink. He yelled at me about leaving dishes in the sink and went off about a few other things.

I reached out to my old friend to talk to him about what had just happened. He informed me that he and his family had moved out of the place we all had previously lived. They had moved to a small mobile home park and said there was a trailer available to rent. I was able to secure it after a short interview and making a deposit.

It is hard to believe but in a period of six months, I had moved my dog and myself a total of five times. We started at my place in Tampa, then the house with a coworker, then my girlfriend's apartment, then my friend's house, and now our own trailer. It had been a stressful time and through it all, I had let my flesh guide me. If I would have had any idea of the amount of stress that I was going to go through, I would have just stayed in Tampa. Those were hard lessons that I learned. The most important being is that you should always talk to God about your decisions and keep it in prayer.

Chapter 29 Takeaway: Moving in the Flesh

I was moving entirely in the flesh. Escaping one reactionary move after another, from one stressful situation to another. How do you keep your focus on God and seek His direction in your life?

Bible verses to reflect upon:
Proverbs 8:34
Hebrews 13:15

Chapter 30

Our Trailer Home

It was my second trailer and strangely enough, it was almost the same size as the one that I was forced to relocate and then had to sell back in the Midwest just a few years earlier.

It was early 2001 and the bar had closed just after New Year's. I then worked at another restaurant and bar for a short time before my sister helped me out with a job from another friend. I had gone through a great deal of stress and turbulence with all the moves and then lost two jobs back to back. The owners of the large nightclub blamed all of us and said we were all fired because of the bar's failure and closing. At the restaurant job, the manager there hired me as a favor to his head bartender who was a friend and customer of mine. However, he did not like me personally or the way I looked, as I had tattoos and my hair down to my waist. My bartending days had ended for the moment but through it all, while employed at the large nightclub, I had stopped drinking by God's grace.

When my girlfriend and I broke up, I was in the midst of all that moving from one place to another. I was emotionally hurt and weighed my options. While with her, I had gotten to where I would only drink one beer if we went out. Our breakup was between Halloween and Thanksgiving. I chose to remain sober and not drink. I cannot say when I drank my last bottle of beer for certain but it was before Thanksgiving.

My sister's friend worked for an order-filling company that filled orders for retail stores. The products that they handled were personal care items of all sorts and prescription drugs. I started in OTC, the over-the-counter department of personal products. The job was fast-paced and demanding. You had to wear a kangaroo pouch-like apron to put each order in as you were selecting it. That weighed on my back and gave me some problems. After I was there a while, I became friends with the night lead of the prescription section. I had to pass an additional background check for security reasons before I could come work in his department. There were narcotics on the property and many cameras covering all areas. The job was much better than the OTC section position. It was a much lighter strain on my back and easier to perform.

Everything was going along just fine until after the September 11th attacks. The company made some changes and brought in a new night manager that wanted a faster-paced production line. That became a problem for me, as I could not keep up with demands. I was required to almost run the entire shift and I just did not have that kind of momentum. I was written up once for not keeping up with the pace that was expected of me. I was not happy and knew I was going to be fired from yet another job if I did not find a way out.

One fateful day I was in the downtown area and heard about a new little bar that had been opened by a former bartender at the large nightclub. I went in and sat down to talk with him, as he was one of the bartenders that I had previously worked for. He had opened the place with two other men and it took a little persuasion but he offered to hire me on full time as a barback.

I went back to the order-pulling job and quit. They were going to fire me in a short while, so I did not give them much notice. The other factor in my quitting was that my job had been located in Tampa, so I had a daily commute. I now had a job in the town I was living in working for an old friend from the nightclub we both used to work at. Things were looking better already on the job front and through all of it; my old friend and his family lived next door to me.

That was an interesting trailer park that sat perhaps on one acre of land and there were four mobile home trailers there. Three regular-size or full-size homes and the small one that Cooper and I had. Times were good for the moment. I was back in the bar business and was not drinking at all. My employment was local and not much of a commute and I had my own place for my dog and me.

God had been good to me and through the years set me free from tobacco, marijuana, hard drugs, and now most recently alcohol. I was struggling in the area of being single though and wanted a woman in my life. I was still having the fight of flesh with pornography.

Chapter 30 Takeaway: A Shift in Direction

God was bringing things into focus as I was praying and talking with Him.

There had been job changes but the moving from place to place was finally over.

How do we keep our focus on God through our trials and triumphs?

Bible verses to reflect upon:
Psalms 37:4
1 Corinthians 14:33

Chapter 31

Next-door Neighbors

The trailer on the corner became available and my friend and his family wanted to move into it, as it was a three-bedroom as opposed to the two-bedroom home they were in. That meant their trailer, which was a full-size two-bedroom home, would open up and I could move over from the small trailer I was in. They moved and I moved, about thirty feet each. The homes were close together but it was nice for a while.

Then my former little trailer was rented out to someone who was a thief and had been to prison. Sometimes people simply do not change. The man stole from the neighbor on the other end of our little park. Things like stereos and other electronics. I believe the only reason he did not break into my house was that I had Cooper.

The man, unfortunately, had a dog and kept it tied up out back to a doghouse. The poor dog used to cry and carry on. It was young and energetic and simply wanted some attention. It was close to my bedroom and because my neighbor was on drugs and drank, he went out often. He also slept through much of the noise his dog made. I called the police several times on noise complaints and some calls were made out of concern for the dog's well being. He only took the dog in on rare occasions and it seemed like it was tied out to its doghouse almost all of the time.

One day, I came home from doing some errands and the man came over and blocked me from getting out of my truck as he leaned over and on the driver's side window and door frame. He asked what kind of stereo I had in my truck and then insisted on borrowing my cell phone to make a call. I downplayed the stereo that was in my truck and let him use my phone. It was unnerving and he was definitely scoping out my truck for a possible break-in. I wound up having an alarm installed at an electronics store, as I did not trust the man at all.

Then one day, I get a call from my landlord asking if I still had a key to the small trailer that the man was living in. I said I think so, let me take a look because I knew I still had one. I had not moved all that long ago and it was a dangerous situation that was unfolding in the neighborhood. The man had stolen some items and was barricaded in the trailer. The police had tracked him down or had followed him home. I went and got the spare key and gave it to my landlord. He opened the door and the police stormed the small trailer and arrested the man. As it turned out, he was on probation and was a repeat offender. He wound up going to prison and I never heard from him again. Afterward, a nice young couple moved in and they were great neighbors from what I remember.

During this time my friendship with my old friend flourished and we had many meals together. We used to go out shopping together and watch movies at their place on their large television. He and his girlfriend's biggest addiction was tobacco. They both smoked cigarettes and they were chain smokers most of the time. I put up with it and was able to tolerate it because at the time in Florida you could smoke in bars. The bar that I worked in was no exception and I used to come home stinking from all the cigarette smoke that I was exposed to. I was still lonely, battling pornography, and wanted to have a girlfriend in my life. I kept praying, as I knew there was a better way than what I kept doing.

Chapter 31 Takeaway:
In Times of Trouble

I began to realize more about the situations we put ourselves in and that are created around us. I prayed for protection for our home and about my neighbor.
How do we pray for others that may be a danger to us?

Bible verses to reflect upon:
Jeremiah 29:11
Matthew 5:44

Chapter 32

She Arrives

One day in May 2003 the woman I would fall deeply in love with walked in. It was a hot evening and the place was packed. There were way too many people for me to get a word in or even approach her that night. My job kept me behind the bar, the long bar where I was at, and then the short bar on the other side of the room that I would help out with too.

What I saw that fateful evening was a beautiful slender woman with long black hair down to her waist. She stood out from all the other women in the bar, she was not like them at all. I was mesmerized by her the instant I saw her. As quickly as she appeared she disappeared and was gone. What was I going to do? The local town had a population of about ninety thousand people and I didn't even know her name.

For the next two weeks, I prayed harder for her to come back to the bar then I had prayed for anything else in a long time. I know I kept asking "God, please send her back to me." Let her come back to the bar and allow me to have a conversation with her. I thought of her every day and prayed that we could meet soon.

On a Thursday evening two weeks later, it was our ladies' night; she walked in and came up to the bar. It was early in the night and we were not crowded, she came in with her friend. I was nervous but spoke with her and when she went to the bathroom, I let her friend know that I liked her and wanted to know more about her. As our conversation continued, I was able to get her phone number and make a date with her. We quickly hit things off by way of talking on the phone and we had our first date at a restaurant a few days later.

We met at the restaurant and after we had our meal, we went back to my place and proceeded to be led by our flesh. We were both extremely attracted to each other. The next day after she went home, she later got back in touch with me and wanted to come back over. Pretty much in an instant, we were now in a relationship. It happened very quickly as those things do. Two lonely people who were attracted to each other and the next thing you know you are in bed.

We dated for a short period of about two weeks before she gave me the news she would be moving about sixty miles away. You see, she was married but was separated and her husband had left her. The place they had been renting, she could not afford by herself. A female friend of hers who lived pretty far away had offered her a place to live.

I remember sitting in my driveway calculating the distance and it was just too great. Here we were in a brand new relationship and she was going to leave. I told her how I felt about her, that I cared for her and did not want her to go. I looked deep within myself and then I asked her to move in with me. She was surprised and then asked me if I was sure. Without hesitation, I said yes. Two weeks into our relationship and she was going to be my live-in girlfriend. It turned out that God does answer prayer and sometimes He gives us exactly what we ask for. I had very much desired to have a girlfriend and here she was.

She was the mother of a teenage daughter and had kind of voluntarily given custody over to her grandmother many years prior. She had some mess in her life with family drama as I would find out but had she moved sixty miles away, it would have taken her further from her family. I also needed to have someone in my life; I was tired of the battle of pornography and loneliness that had plagued me for many years.

Here we were, two people brought together and we were determined to make it work. I was still at the bar and that would continue through the summer. She drank when she would go out and one night she got drunk. She got sick by the bed and I took care of her. I told her afterward that I could not handle that kind of drunkenness. She had come to my bar and I now know after the fact, that my bartender friend slipped her something in her drink. I did not find out until afterward but that is what contributed to her condition that night.

Things changed after that, she realized that I loved her and cared for her. She did not drink as much or as often and then the weekend of my birthday I got an unexpected gift. The bar announced that they were closing. Telltale signs were leading up to this with low liquor supplies, which happened at the previous large nightclub too. It was September 2003 and I was now out of work again from the bar business.

I decided I had had enough of the bar business. I had spent five years behind the counter as a barback, bartender, and barback once again. God had heard my cries to become sober and that was accomplished while at the large nightclub. He had answered my prayers about bringing my girlfriend and me together. It was time to look to a new industry and profession.

Chapter 32 Takeaway:
God Answers Prayer

I had been praying for a girlfriend to come into my life for a couple of years.
God answered my prayer and had brought us together.
How do you stay faithful in your prayer life each day?

Bible verses to reflect upon:
Psalms 27:14
Hebrews 11:6

Chapter 33

New Beginnings

The funny thing about starting over is sometimes you end up going back to what you know. I had been to two audio colleges and wound up in office work then the bar circuit because I could not find any audio work other than unpaid internships.

I took a job in food distribution that was similar to the OTC job that I had a couple of years prior. I was an order selector and worked in the warehouse on the night crew. Things were fine until one day; the manager informed me that I would now be working in the freezer unit. That was not pleasing to hear as I quickly found out; they kept the temperature at zero. You read that correctly. They supplied a snowmobile suit, hat, and gloves to do the work but I did not last long in that position. As I recall, I worked one week in those conditions and quit without notice. I had not moved to central Florida to freeze to death in some warehouse.

I had made some friends as a bartender and one of those friends was a stagehand. I reached out to him and with my background, I was hired on by the company he worked for. My first gig with them was at the local convention center in town. I had lived in town for three years and did not even know there was such a place. They had an arena and I was working on an ice show on my first assignment. I looked around and walked around when I could. I then asked around about employment. It did not take long to go through the hiring process and before the end of the year I was hired as a technician at the local convention center. Praise God!

All those years later and I was finally employed in the industry I had gone to college for. It was classified as a part-time job but it came with full-time hours for most of the year. That turned out to be a huge blessing. There was a theater, arena, two large convention halls, a ballroom, and several meeting rooms. I was exposed to many things on the technical side while working in that large venue. I had a background in electricity from high school and had been to an audiovisual college then to a second audio college. My work life was coming together and it felt like I might have a career.

Things at home were good with my girlfriend but there was tension building between my old college friend's girlfriend and my own. I do not recall the exact timing of the decline but it was early on. My girlfriend as I would soon find out like most women had a disdain for women who were strippers. My once close friends started to slip away as there was a wedge between our girlfriends.

Sometimes in life situations arise and people are forced to choose sides and they do. We were still friends but we did not hang out together and it was kind of weird. He had his girlfriend; her two kids and they had a child together shortly before my girlfriend and I came together as a couple. None of us were married to each other but we were both in serious relationships. We kept things on a casual friendship level. He and I missed hanging out together but we did the best we could in the situation we were in.

I spent my time working then being home with her and Cooper. She had gone back to work in retail the first year that we were together. She worked at a clothing store in the women's section as a sales clerk. Life was going along and things were good until a couple of things happened.

Our neighborhood was not good and was getting worse. One day I came home and my friend informed me that just four doors down someone had been shot dead at their front door. There had been prostitutes hanging around by the school corner and drug dealers throughout the neighborhood. The shooting was related to drugs and that was the turning point for me. I began to see what it would take to buy a place and move us out of the declining area.

The other thing that happened, was my girlfriend started having pain in her legs and hurting all over. She went to her doctor and proceeded to be diagnosed with fibromyalgia. She had to stop working retail because of the pain that would not allow her to stand for hours on end. She started working from home selling things on eBay. Back then it was a booming marketplace and we both made money as I too sold things that I had for many years. Old toys, sports cards, and I also got into selling T-shirts from working as a stagehand for arena rock shows in the Tampa and Orlando markets.

We were doing all right financially but my credit was still being repaired from defaulting on my student loans. I was in a repayment program but my credit was slow to come back to a high enough score to purchase anything. We had to stay there a while longer as I did positive things to build my credit score back up. It is a long road back to good credit once you default on your student loans. God was helping us align things to prepare for a move.

Chapter 33 Takeaway: God is Faithful

God had blessed me with a new job that would use my skills and become a career.
He was giving me guidance on preparing for buying a home.
How do you praise and thank God for what He has done in your life?

Bible verses to reflect upon:
Psalms 34:1
Acts 16:25

Chapter 34

Coming Into Focus

By this point, my girlfriend and I were in love with each other. She meant the world to me and I would have done just about anything for her. I was working two jobs, one as a stagehand and the other as a technician.

On my technician job at the convention center, the pay scale was on the low side, as it was city-owned and operated. My manager liked me and another technician that was hired about the same time. He allowed us to test up to the next level then another level. I had been a Technician I, Technician II, and then a Show Technician. It was nice of him to allow me to do that and make more money.

Things came into focus at the end of 2005 for us as we found a house located in a country suburb that we both liked. God had blessed me with plenty of work and a woman who loved me. Now we had a place far away from prostitutes, the neighborhood drug dealers, and shootings that had occurred. We moved into the home in January of 2006 and were just moving forward in many ways. I was working much of the time and had a housewife even though we were not married. We were engaged though and I intended to marry her. Just a few months into the year the following events unfolded.

One day, I came to work and the strangest thing happened. My boss, the assistant manager to who I reported directly to was out from work and I only got fragmented pieces of the story of what happened from several people. Remember this was a part-time job and I was not there every day.

He had been dating a woman who worked with us but in a different department. They were both drinkers and on the Saturday night that had just passed, something bad happened between them. He shot her with a handgun, not once but twice. He shot her in the shoulder and then in the foot. He claimed it was an accidental discharge while cleaning the weapon in the home. She somehow escaped and called the police, while he left. He fled the scene but she was unaware of that fact.

The police came, the SWAT team came, and then they proceed to tear gas his house. When they finally stormed his house, they found that it was empty. The local newspaper put all of that on the front page of the Sunday paper because he was now a wanted and armed fugitive. Shortly after that, he turned himself in and then had to go through all of the court proceedings even though she refused to press charges. The state of Florida stepped right in and charged him though. He lost his job after the verdict came down. He did not go to prison but was extremely bitter about being let go by the city.

Now, there was an opening for his position. I took it upon myself to step up my efforts at work in the hopes of being promoted to the position. During the process of trying to replace him, I was tasked with the duty of training new hires. It took me a moment but I asked if I could become a Supervisor. That would put me at the highest level of our department's part-time positions. I was granted that request and then began to reap the rewards of my hard work.

I also stopped working the stagehand job because of working sixty to sixty-five hours a week on the job. I was paid hourly and received overtime, being gone much of the time from home but was truly blessed financially. I felt as though I was walking in the right direction with God and He was opening doors for me. I was thankful to be where I was at that moment.

Chapter 34 Takeaway: Preparing the way

It had been a long hard road but God was showing me a couple of key things.
He is my provider and He cares for me.
How do you keep your eyes on God?

Bible verses to reflect upon:
Psalms 37:3
1 John 5:14-15

Chapter 35

Marriage

As we settled into our new home, my fiancé was still married to another man. I had not met him as he had been out of the picture since day one of her and me being together. He found her though, as he too wanted to marry another woman. My fiancé was not happy about having to go before a judge but was happy to be divorcing her husband who had been gone for three years.

It was approaching summertime and the day came when she had to go to court. I went with her to keep her calm and offer emotional support if she needed it. Their marriage had been over a long time and it was a formality in her eyes. When they went in, I sat in the hallway and waited. She came out a few moments later and it was done. It was a simple divorce as they had no children together and each had all of their own belongings. My fiancé took back her maiden name and got a new driver's license.

I will admit in hindsight, that we should have waited a little while after her divorce to get married. However, according to the Bible, our whole relationship was done in reverse order. We got married shortly after this, in July 2006 we became husband and wife. We went to the beach for our honeymoon and sent out wedding announcements to family members. My family was shocked that we had done a simple justice of the peace wedding ceremony at the courthouse.

You see, I was her third husband and she did not want a traditional church wedding with a pastor, nor did she want a white wedding dress. I went along with her request because I loved her more than I had ever loved any woman I had been with. My mother was disappointed in our choice, she was happy that we were married, just not how it was carried out.

Right before this, in the month prior I was given the position of assistant manager at work. It had come down to just one other candidate who also worked on our crew. He did not have the experience I had, nor had he stepped up to do all the work that I had done. Since I picked up much of the slack and helped out my manager, he chose me for the position.

I know God worked it out as I was praying about things and I felt, we had finally done the right thing and had become husband and wife. The happiness I felt was going to be short-lived though. I was hourly and had been making all of that overtime. I was now going to be salary at about the same hourly wage. That meant no more overtime, as I would be paid for a forty-hour workweek. I am sure many of you know the joy and the pain of being in a salary position.

The estimated tax bill for our new home arrived in the mail the first week of August. It was not good news, since I had purchased the home in January I could not file for a homestead exception and the tax bill had gone up drastically. At that time I remember sharing the news with my wife and asking her to go back to work part-time or to get back into selling on eBay. Since I had been making really good money up until that point, she had stopped doing much of anything to bring money in. That was fine during that particular time but now I was on salary and our biggest bill had just gone up drastically. That conversation did not go well and there was resistance on her part at the time.

With the added financial stress, I looked to my old stagehand job and sought to make some money on the side with that when I could. That job was dependent mostly on concerts but I was able to work some corporate events as they were called. Those were hotel-meeting events, the pay was better and it was much like the work I had been doing on my regular job.

During that time, my wife did go thrift store shopping and would find hidden treasures and then turn around and sell them online for a profit. While I was gone much of the time, my wife wanted to get a pet of her own. My dog Cooper hated cats and that was her preferred pet. One day she went to the animal shelter and adopted a young energetic female dog that had been abused. She named her Baley and we now had two dogs.

Chapter 35 Takeaway: A Good Home Life

God had blessed me with a home and a wife.
Happiness would be short-lived though.
How do you pray when things appear to be good in your life?

Bible verses to reflect upon:
Proverbs 18:22
Ephesians 5:25

_____

_____

_____

_____

_____

_____

_____

_____

_____

_____

_____

_____

Chapter 36

Troubles

With our moving now months behind us, we left the troubled neighborhood and my friend and his family behind. It had not been easy for me to disconnect from him, as we had been friends for over a decade. As the fall season came upon us with slightly cooler temperatures and the end of hurricane season, a dramatic series of events occurred.

Remember my pornography addiction? It had been lying dormant while I was with my girlfriend, fiancé, and now wife. We had an active sex life most of our relationship up until we got married. There was a mental shift in our relationship though when we got married.

I believe I expected certain things to be done as in a partnership and she had her own ideas as well. I was her third husband, so she had been down this road before. One of the key things that fed into my addiction at the time was taking photos of my wife. She sold many women's clothing items of all kinds online and was the perfect model. After getting married our sex life took a dramatic downturn and at the time, I did not understand why. I was still myself and loved her more than any other woman I had ever been with. What was going on?

Prior to us moving, it would have been in the fall of 2005, one day she announced to me that she was going to set up an account on MySpace. That was before Facebook went public. I still remember when she said that, a chill went down my spine and I heard in the spirit "no good will come from it."

She wanted to reconnect with her biological father and other long, lost family members. I tried to gently talk her out of this but she had made up her mind. It was about a year after she opened her account and she had been meeting people online. Those were dangerous grounds for a married woman or man to be exploring online.

One day we went shopping at a large grocery store and I was not expecting the following to happen. We were in a canned goods area of an isle and there was another couple in front of us. The woman had on a midriff tank top with what we used to call Daisy Dukes jean shorts. To be polite, she was showing a whole lot of skin. I could not help myself and I stared intently at her. My wife noticed but did not say anything until after we left the store.

Once we got into our vehicle, she asked me about looking at the other woman. I downplayed it the best that I could but admitted that I looked simply because of how she was dressed. Looking back, I was trying to blame the woman. Once we got home and unpacked the groceries, when I tried to get close to her, she then asked me if I wanted the other woman. It seems that I had profoundly hurt my wife emotionally and had not intended to do so. It did not take long for her to turn from me and turn to another man.

What had I done wrong? I looked or lusted after another woman in front of my wife. That was wrong and I should not have done it. Not because I got caught but because it was wrong. I had no idea at the time what a problem I had with pornography, looking and lusting after the flesh. I did not speak to the woman, I did not get her name or her number, and nothing was said. With one look I had ruined my marriage? It sure does not seem like we were ever on stable ground, does it?

It took just a few weeks but she met a man on MySpace and they were then chatting online. I know that they began to text and talk as well. I was still working full time with the city and then one weekend, she started going over to a girlfriend's and spending time away from home. This was a woman I did not know, a friend from before we got together. The first time that happened, she came home at 2 AM and equated it to closing time at the bar.

When she started coming home at 5 and 6 AM, I knew something was going on. She did not want to spend Thanksgiving together either but we did. She also claimed she was going out with this female friend of hers. My suspicions accelerated when she would not give me the name, address, or phone number of the woman. The other clear sign was that we were no longer having sex at all.

In addition, my mother wanted to come down for the Christmas holiday, as she had not seen our new place. Her birthday was also three days before Christmas. When I took my vacation that week, my wife was gone. She refused to be home with me and I had no idea where she was staying. I knew things were bad but I had no idea just how bad they were. I was worried and stressed out; she would not take my calls and then would only call back if she felt like it much later.

When my mother came for her visit, I was a wreck and shared with her the little information that I knew. I believe that was my first time of fasting from food but it was stress-related. I had no appetite and when my wife and I did talk she was cold and callous towards me on the phone. My wife came home to keep up appearances on that Friday, which also happened to be my mother's birthday. She was not home long and I asked her if we go into the bedroom for a moment to talk. She agreed but it quickly turned ugly, as she would not tell me where or with whom she was staying. That only lasted a moment and she quickly left as she could tell that I was emotionally hurting and she was hiding something serious from me. She was nervous and did not want to be there or with me at all.

My mother's trip to see us was pretty disastrous, largely due to my wife's absence and secrecy. My mother had compassion and sympathy towards me during her visit. It was the worst Christmas I had perhaps ever had.

Chapter 36 Takeaway: Looking and Lusting

Looking leads to lusting and when you are married you should only desire your spouse. Our problems came to light quickly after we were married.
How do you seek God in times of trouble in your marriage?

Bible verses to reflect upon:
Proverbs 3:5-6
Ephesians 4:31-32

Chapter 37

Divorce

One day, I received an email notice from eBay. My wife had been selling on the site for several years with my account, which was still active at the time. There were certain items that she had flagged for search results. If someone listed that particular item, we would get an email alert that it was for sale. As I was looking at that one email, I saw a slender woman with long black hair modeling some pants. I instantly recognized her as my wife. I looked at the seller's name and info and it was no one that I had ever heard of.

I told one of my closest friends at work about it and he said to keep watching if they listed anything else besides women's clothing. A short time later, the mystery man and my wife listed some books and other items for sale. My friend had an eBay account and made a purchase. The day came for the package to arrive. There in the upper left-hand corner was the return mailing address in my wife's handwriting.

We wasted no time and my friend drove me to the address. There, in the carport was my wife's car. No other vehicles were at the house. It was a cold rainy day in late December as we sat out on the side of the road. I was so worked up emotionally at that moment; it was an intense adrenaline rush. My friend asked me if I wanted to go up to the house but because I was so shaken I said no and took some pictures with the camera that I had brought. His house and her car that was in the carport and we quickly left, I had caught her.

I knew where she was and had the man's name and address. All of that information came from a simple forgotten notification setting that sent me that one email from a search alert. As stressful as it was, at least I now knew where she was. I do not recall exactly when she came home to get clothes but it was close to New Year's Eve. I confronted her in a calm tone, as it happened in our bedroom. I let her know that I knew she was with him. I said his name and she was shocked. She was more stunned by it; she could not believe that I had caught her. I had her in a tough spot in the conversation but I loved her and asked her to come home. I said we can work it out but you have to end it and come home. She was upset and did not want to talk any further about anything. She said no to coming home and to us working things out, she took some of her clothes and left.

The next time we spoke, it was about her coming and getting her things out of the house. There was a whole lot of stress involved with the process but I believe she had some friends come help her while I was at work. I had said that I did not want him, her new man in my house and to please just get your stuff out while I am at work. It was an extremely stressful situation for us both.

I will not go into all the details of the divorce but I chose to file against her because she was cheating on me with another man. Then, she chose the boyfriend when I gave her a chance to come home and work things out. I had been willing to forgive her and work on the marriage. She wanted no part of it. My marriage was about to be over legally and the sad part of it was, we were still in what some people call the honeymoon phase.

We were married in July and she started seeing the other man in November. The looking at another woman incident happened in late October of that year. Five months into our marriage and it was over. I was in shock during that period of time. By the time the court date happened in early March 2007, I had lost thirty pounds. The day I saw my wife for the last time at court, she actually looked terrible. She was really thin and strangely enough looked as stressed as I had felt. She was angry and upset with me that day and snapped at me when I simply tried to talk to her.

Divorce is a terrible thing; thank God we had no children together. We chose to do a simple divorce, I had my belongings and she had hers. I had purchased the house as a single man without her name or credit rating. She said she did not want any part of it and for me to keep it. I also wound up keeping the dog she adopted as her boyfriend had at least one cat and could not have a large dog in his home.

Looking back at our marriage, we both made mistakes and on that final court day when the judge's ruling came down, she may have been even sadder than I. She now had three failed marriages under her belt and had lost a good man. I was not perfect by any means but I loved her and cared for her more than any other woman I had been with and she knew it.

Chapter 37 Takeaway: Times of Sadness

I had lost my best friend, my companion, and my wife to another man.

There were many negative emotions and I should have relied on God.

How do you keep your eyes upon the Lord when you are suffering?

Bible verses to reflect upon:
Psalms 25:4-5
James 1:12

Chapter 38

My Best Friend

My dog Cooper had been with me through many trying times and moves. I adopted him in 1994 when my life was in serious distress with my drug use and court battles at the time. He was just a scrawny puppy; perhaps four months old back then.

The dog was my companion, my guardian, and my best friend. We had been through so much together. One day, I came home from work and he was lying on the living room floor. He could not move and he had excess fluid in his stomach. I had to pick him up; he was a solid seventy pounds. Have you ever had to pick up a dead weight? It felt like he weighed twice that but I managed to get him out to my truck and put him in through the rear hatch area.

I do not recall taking Baley with me to the vet, as she was young and energetic. I had to crate train her after my wife left because of her energy, she would be destructive while I was at work. I had never done that kind of training before but when some of my furniture got partially destroyed it was time. We went to my vet and they said that the attention that he needed required an animal hospital. I went as fast as I could and had to leave him there for testing.

I went back home to be with Baley and wait for the call. I also phoned my manager to let him know what was going on with my dog. He had been supportive through the divorce process. During the recently passed Christmas season, after my mom went back home I worked fifty to sixty hours a week. I did not have to, I was salary and he understood I did not want to be home without my wife.

I get the call, it was around 10 PM, and they said he had a cyst. It was a cancerous cyst that had ruptured and he was bleeding to death internally. I knew there was only one option. I went to the hospital to be with him, the vet on duty was a woman and she was so kind. She told me to remember the good times, not this. He was in a kennel bed and had an IV in his front leg. They had given him pain meds to make him comfortable.

As I walked into the room, his long tail waged ever so slightly. He was happy to see me and I was him, just not like that. I went over and held him in my lap. I petted him on his head and just loved on him for as long as I could. The vet looked over at me as I had tears streaming down my face. I gave her the head nod of yes and she came and administered the drug that put him to sleep into his IV. I cried and cried as I felt him slip away. He had been with me for over twelve years. I held him until his body temperature started to drop, I don't know how long that was but he was my best friend and I held on as long as I could.

I made arrangements for a private cremation and picked out an urn the next day. I was devastated, just the week prior my divorce had been finalized. It was as if he knew that I needed him through the separation and divorce process. Once those were done, perhaps he knew it was all right for him to pass on.

There is something special I want to share. My dog had parvo (parvovirus) as a puppy after I adopted him. I hand-fed him rice and skinless, boneless chicken meat and nursed him through it and back to health. He was near death but made it. I was living in the party house at that time. Then two years later I was living out at my dad's place and he came down with heartworms for the second time.

I had a local vet and the man lied to me about the treatment that he was going to administer. I later found out, he almost killed my dog by injecting arsenic into his heart. This was a common treatment at the time but he did lie to me about another treatment. It was only afterward that I found out the truth.

My dog had depended on me when he went through some serious illnesses when he was younger. When we were living in the trailer in Florida before my ex-wife came into our lives something special happened one night. I had let him sleep in the bed with me after all of our moves and we finally had a place of our own again. Previously, he had been with me in that deeply spiritual and special dream sequence from God at my sister's house.

On that night he and I shared another dream. He was running free and frolicking through a pasture with a farmhouse close by. There were trees and a stream; he went to the stream to get a drink. I was not near him but was instantly worried about alligators. He proceeded to get his drink from the stream and I woke up. There were no alligators as it was a pleasant dream. When I awoke, he awoke; he looked over at me and licked my face.

That is one of many pleasant memories I have of Cooper. He was a great companion and guardian and I will always love him. Thank you, God, for our time together.

Chapter 38 Takeaway: Good Memories

I had gone through much heartache in a short time.
I refused to go back to what I had been set free from.
When heartache comes, how do you stay focused on God?

Bible verses to reflect upon:
Isaiah 49:13
Matthew 5:4

Chapter 39

Times of Music

I decided to go to work for a new stagehand company, as they had split from the original one that I had previously been working for.

When I caught up with the woman that ran the crew of stagehands at those shows, I was able to tell her what had happened to me in the previous months. She looked at me and said, "Gee Shane, your life sounds like a sad, old country song." My wife left me, my dog died and I had been on an all-stress diet that saw me drop thirty pounds in sixty days. It made me laugh when she said that, it was good to be out and about again. God's grace and mercy were upon me in the midst of the heartache.

I had a musician friend from work and we started playing music together shortly after all of that. It was good to be creative again, as during my time with my ex-wife I had put music on the back burner. I did nothing musically the whole time we were together. That was what I chose to do, as her second husband had been a guitarist trying to make music work as well. I knew it was a thorn in her side or perhaps just a painful reminder of her former husband.

I became focused on music with my friend from work during that time. He and I wrote the better part of an album of original songs. It was a mix of hard rock, heavy metal, and jazz-folk styles of music. I wrote most of the lyrics, played rhythm guitar, and sang vocals. My friend played rhythm and lead guitar and would sing some of the backup vocals.

There were many months of playing and writing music together. It lasted most of the year. We would usually get together once or twice a week. We had gotten to the point where we were talking about adding a bass guitar player. We even had aspirations of putting a full band together, maybe being a five-piece band with bass guitar, drums, and keyboard. By the time we got about an album's worth of material recorded we wound up going our separate ways.

Previously he had been a seminary student and had a different view of God when he eventually dropped out of that program. He was a believer but we had different views about God and things that can happen in the spirit world. When I tried to share some of my first-hand experiences of what I had gone through, it was simply too much for him. Our friendship just kind of ended. That saddened me but sometimes people come into your life for just one season. Where one ends, another begins.

Chapter 39 Takeaway: Praise the Lord

I now had some happiness in my life by writing and playing music. I had come through the valley and was at a peak in my life. How do you praise God through your peaks and valleys?

Bible verses to reflect upon:
Psalms 34:1
Hebrews 13:15

_____
_____
_____
_____
_____
_____
_____
_____
_____
_____
_____
_____
_____

Chapter 40

Old Friends and Music

My old friend and his wife came to mind once my divorce was final and with Cooper's passing, I needed to talk to someone. I still had both of their phone numbers and I reached out to him. He was glad to hear from me and we planned on getting together. They too had moved and were out in the country, in the next county over. They had also grown tired of the crime in the old neighborhood and left.

Our first get-together was at their place and then they came out to look at the place I had bought just a year prior. While I was with my ex-wife, she did not want to do anything with the house. The previous owners had whitewashed with a sprayer just about every room in the house. Once she was gone, the first thing that I did was go pick out some paint and I started painting throughout the house. My friend and his family came over and helped me rebuild the back sun deck. It was a good size deck that was twelve feet deep by twenty-one feet wide. Many boards were rotted and needed to be replaced, so it turned into a big job. I was thankful for the help and to reconnect with my old friend and his family.

One day at work a man approached me as I was in the hallway of our arena. He said he had seen me around and he too worked nearby the convention center. He asked me about audio and mixing sound. I told him that I had much experience in that field and then he proceeded to tell me that he had a band and they needed a soundman. They were getting ready to start playing out, while the singer and drummer had experience in sound, they could not mix audio and perform at the same time.

I met with them at their rehearsal space and they could quickly tell that I was an experienced soundman. I knew my way around the soundboard and the rack gear that they had. The next step was to come and do a live show with them. That would include helping them set up, mix the show as the soundman and then help tear down when they were done performing. I hit it out of the park at that first gig. They were impressed with my mixing skills and the drummer was smiling ear to ear when he looked at me and said, "You're hired!" Just like that, I had a part-time sound gig and some new friends. It was a perfect fit for me as it helped keep my audio skills polished. God was blessing me with new friends and a rekindled passion for music.

There had been another major change during the year that happened at work. The man who had originally hired me, and had been my manager promoting me through several positions at the convention center retired. When he announced this, several people applied, including myself and two other people from our crew. I had only been the assistant manager for about a year at that point and upper management decided to go with an outside hire. They hired a man who was a traveling soundman from a famous circus.

He had advanced audio skills and had been a world traveler, setting up sound systems in all kinds of settings and venues across the globe. When he started at the convention center, my sound duties became much less as he shifted my focus more to the administrative side of our business. That was a welcome change and would eventually help me grow as a manager. I continued to stay the course with work and music; however, more changes were coming my way.

Chapter 40 Takeaway: A Chance to Grow

Having doors open and close in a season of change gave me a chance to grow.
How do you thank God when He opens or closes doors in your life?

Bible verses to reflect upon:
Psalms 9:10
Colossians 3:15

Chapter 41

Workplace Dating

There is something to be said for the number forty. Jesus and Moses both fasted forty days in the Bible. The flood occurred because it rained for forty days and forty nights. What I am about to tell you was a key moment in my life at age forty. There is a saying that had been around a long time "don't date in the workplace". That was a lesson that I was about to learn for myself the hard way.

There was a woman that I was attracted to at work. She worked in a different department but we still worked in the same building. One day we were talking in the theater and she told me she was going to have her breasts enlarged. She was a petite woman as she was short and had a small frame. I complimented her and said she looked good just as she was. She smiled, said thank you and that she was going to do that because she wanted to.

A little while later, I asked her if she would like to go out on a date. We wound up going back to her place, talking for hours. It did not take long for us to go to bed together as we were both physically attracted to one another. That turned into a relationship rather quickly. She had also previously dated someone in her department but they had gone their separate ways.

The timing of this relationship was premature and we both jumped right in. She decided, that we could save money if we moved in together. It seemed as though she was ready to come live with me as her ex-boyfriend had some stalker characteristics in him. He kept showing up at her place and would not leave her alone and they still worked together. I thought since she wanted to be with me and get away from him, that her moving in would be a good move for both of us. Here again, I was not praying about those things but being driven by the flesh.

The day came and we moved her in. She had a traditional truck with a full-size bed and I had my truck with its hatchback. We were now living together. She was a hard worker and helped me with projects around the house. The painting that I had wanted to do, helping out with yard work and whatever else she could assist with. We worked slightly different schedules and would drive separately most days. We would have lunch together often and things were good most of the time.

Then the day came and we had a blowout argument. I do not recall what it was all about, I just remember making up with her and getting her a card and flowers. She had given up her own place willingly but had sacrificed some things to come and live with me. I believe some of that resurfaced at that time. I was starting to see the truth in that old saying about workplace dating. Things continued forward in our relationship again until one day, some insecurities came out of her that I had not expected.

It was on a weekend and I was working as the soundman for the band. I was now being paid and I considered it a part-time job. The band was performing and as the sound engineer, there are adjustments that I would do for each song. When the guitarist would play a lead or solo, I would push his volume up and when he was done, I would bring his volume back down. That is one of the elements of mixing sound. It is a process. While I was doing that, she looked at me rather angrily and said, "You are supposed to be paying attention to me."

I quickly explained to her what I was doing and went on with my duties that evening. More insecurities later came out and our relationship started to be chipped away by them. We began the journey together about one year after my divorce. I thought I was ready but then she would point certain things out to me that proved otherwise.

There was another argument after that and I do not recall what it was about. It was what she said to me that stuck with me. Afterward, she looked at me and said, "What did she do to you? You're broken." That was a reference to my emotional state at that time in our relationship. It made me think about my ex-wife and everything that I had gone through.

I found out later in our relationship, that my girlfriend had three children in total. I did not know why she kept it from me for the length of time that she did. The youngest lived with his dad in another state and the two older ones, a boy and girl, were living nearby. Her daughter was her oldest, then her first-born son. The daughter was nineteen and was about to be out on her own. Her son was close behind, as he had just turned eighteen. These kids had been out of her life for several if not many years. My girlfriend had an assorted drug past and had lost them to the state years ago.

The timing of all that was peculiar to me. I saw red flags everywhere and she did not. These two young adults were looking for a place to live and decided to reconnect with their mother. I agreed to meet them, as my girlfriend was very emotional about her two oldest children wanting to come live with her. They came to the house one afternoon and we sat and talked. I mostly listened. I could not get past the fact that these two had not talked to their mother.

The boy had just turned eighteen and wanted out of where he was and he was jobless. The young woman was employed as she was staying with her father who was nearby. Things were not going well for her there. I simply saw red flags and more red flags in those situations. By state law, once you allow someone to move in, to get him or her out, you just about have to evict them. What had I gotten myself into?

After they left, things got incredibly worse between her and me. I said I had to think about it. I had a three-bedroom home, so we could have made room for them. I reached out to my dad for advice as he and I had a renewed relationship since I had moved to Florida a decade earlier. His advice resounded clearly with my own gut instincts.

I then had to have the very unpleasant conversation of not letting them move in with us. I proceeded to point out to her that these two were complete strangers to me as well as her, had fallen on deaf ears. There was an argument that unfolded and our relationship came to an end. She moved out and got an apartment that was large enough for the three of them. Sadly, later on, my suspicions proved to be true as there was drug use and then thievery surrounding these two young adults. I understood why she left, she was their mother and a mother's love is strong and unconditional.

Now the part of dating in the workplace would come full circle. There was tension between us, then she went back to her ex-boyfriend that still worked there, and lastly, she helped her daughter get a job there too. There was much drama around me; I would have been wiser to have adhered to the old saying of "don't date in the workplace." When we allow our flesh to rule our lives, those are the kinds of things that can and will happen.

Chapter 41 Takeaway: Heed the Warning

Here I was again in a relationship that was completely driven by my flesh.
I was not walking after the spirit but instead after the flesh.
How do you keep your flesh in check and seek after God?

Bible verses to reflect upon:
Proverbs 6:25
1 John 2:16

Chapter 42

Dogs and God

In December 2008 after she left and right before Christmas, I woke up one morning and the left side of my face was sagging. I could not move it. I could not even talk right. I do not recall talking to my manager but I am sure that I made a quick call to him, as it was a workday.

I went straight to my doctor and just walked in. I really could not talk well at all. The receptionist took one look at me and said, "Have a seat." She was going to alert the doctor and quickly have me examined. It was a serious condition and normally it would take at least two weeks to get an appointment with my doctor.

Upon looking at me, he quickly determined that I had come down with Bells Palsy. He asked me about my personal life and through slurred speech, I told him about the events that had recently played out. Without hesitation, he diagnosed my condition directly related to stress. I had to take a couple of different medicines and he kept a close eye on me with checkups for a few weeks. My quick reaction to just go to him and be under his care turned things in my favor.

I thankfully had no lasting results from that and in a short time, my face returned to normal. That was one of the scariest medical conditions in a physical sense that I have ever had in my life. During my recovery time while at home, I spent all of it with my two dogs.

One of the good things that came from my previous relationship was that we adopted a dog. We went to the local pound and chose a cute but kind of sad-looking dog in a single kennel and brought him home for Baley and us. I had Baley from my ex-wife, adopting her from the pound. When we separated she signed ownership over to me. Then my oldest companion Cooper passed away. Baley was young, energetic, and needed a playmate. Our new dog was a mixed breed and we named him Roscoe. He was a medium-sized dog, Beagle, Boxer, and perhaps a touch of Ridgeback in him. He was truly one of a kind.

After my girlfriend left and as I was recovering from my condition, I realized something was missing. I had been living life on my terms and things were not working out well for me during that time.

One morning, I came across a program that my old college friend had shared with me years earlier. It was a preaching-teaching Bible study program. An older pastor who had been a veteran, a farmer, and a pilot sat behind a plain wooden desk and taught from the Bible. I was intrigued by him, how he talked and taught the Bible. I had seen many religious preachers on television; most had a flash or a flare to them. They also almost always asked for money.

The man had no flash, he did not ask for money but what he did have was passion. He came across as a salt-of-the-earth kind of man. He taught God's Word plain and simple. He would read from The Holy Bible, chapter-by-chapter, verse-by-verse. They would also put the scriptures up on the screen for you to read along with. He would then relate it to things that he had seen in his lifetime as well as the things that were currently happening in our world.

The teaching portion of the program was thirty minutes and then the later thirty minutes was the question and answer time. People would write in, send in letters through the mail and ask whatever they wanted about God's Word. The man was amazing and the only thing that was ever off the table for discussion was talking about other pastors and churches. He answered questions with Biblical reference and guidance.

I quickly fell in love with the program and watched it every day before work. I had done away with cable television due to the high cost and terrible programming choices and had installed an aerial antenna. I was able to pick up many channels in central Florida and a surprising number of Christian channels. I was blessed to have the program on at 5 AM on one channel and 6 AM on another. It was a one-hour program and between the two different time slots, I would be spiritually fed each morning before work. Praise God!

The program is what drew me back to God. I mean completely back. Program after program, I looked forward to each morning Monday through Friday. He had two sons that were in the ministry as well. The oldest would fill in from time to time for his dad. However, it was just not the same when the senior pastor was out.

It was the program though that got me interested in God's Word again. Developing a relationship with the Lord. I even purchased materials from them by donation, to go deeper into the Word, to study and grow as a Christian. I had found a church after many years of being away from one. It was a television church but the pastor always said, "When you're here, you're in church." God will reach you where you are.

Chapter 42 Takeaway: The Word of God

There is nothing like discovering or perhaps rediscovering God's Word.
I was the latter, renewed, energized, and excited about God and His Word.
Do you have a daily routine for reading the Bible?

Bible verses to reflect upon:
Psalms 119:9
2 Peter 1:4

Chapter 43

Second Chances and Endings

Sometimes, we just don't want to let go. In the spring of 2009, my dad had come down to visit and we did some roofing repair work and installed new doors on the home. I had talked to my old friend and needed to borrow some power tools. He was willing to help me out, so we traveled out to his place in the next county over and had a short visit. When we were done with the work, my dad returned home and I returned my friend's tools to him. That would be the last time I ever saw him.

I did not know it at the time; however, over the last two years of visiting with them periodically I had found out some disturbing things. She had been a stripper for a long time but after they moved to a different county her profession changed. She started making adult films on an amateur regional level. My friend had been a video engineer and had previously worked in television. He was now using his skills to film adult movies. That was the main reason they had moved out of the old neighborhood. It was legal in the county they were now in to engage in those activities. The secondary reason they left was because of crime and safety.

I was not comfortable with any of it and as I was growing closer and deeper with God, they were going deeper into the darkness of sexual sin. He was my friend long before she came along, however for a few years there were both my friends. The separation and then ending of our friendship was indeed painful. God was separating them from me; only at the time, I was not aware of that. I would call and leave voicemails as I thought maybe we could get something to eat once in a while but I was wrong in thinking that and attempting to do so. God had shut that door and no one can open a door that He has shut.

Then my ex-girlfriend with the three children came back into my life. I had sympathy and compassion for her. Things had not gone well with the two older children that as I suspected, took advantage of her and had made for a terrible and stressful home life. Her boyfriend whom she dated before me and after me had his own problems and was kind of an immature individual most of the time. I opened myself back up and let her move in once again, this time as a roommate not as a girlfriend. That was what some people today would describe as, "It's complicated"

It was a mistake on my part. She lived with me for around five months and left towards the end of summer in mid-August. There was drama at work, drama with her on-again, off-again boyfriend, and drama with the kids. Too many things to even write about. I had for a brief moment thought we could be together again after she moved back in. My thinking in that was wrong and thankfully that did not happen. It is truly rare for a couple to get back together and for things to work out. Most of the time it is better to leave that door closed. God was cleaning my house and slowly preparing me for the future.

Chapter 43 Takeaway: Purging

As you grow in the Lord, some things will need to be removed or added to your life.
I was going through that process and was renewing my mind with the Word of God.
Do you listen to the Holy Spirit for these directions in your life?

Bible verses to reflect upon:
Isaiah 59:19
Galatians 5:1

Chapter 44

Dating

You might have thought after all the drama with the last girlfriend that I would have been done with women for a while. That was not the case at all. I had started to explore dating websites while she was still living with me as a roommate. During that time, I still had a strong sexual desire and pornography problem.

I wanted a girlfriend for several reasons. I did not want to be alone, I wanted companionship and I wanted to have a sex life. What I was missing physically and emotionally was my ex-wife and the relationship that we once had. I was trying to fill that void with another woman.

Since I did not drink, going to bars and nightclubs did not appeal to me at all. So, I turned to dating websites for finding a girlfriend. There were many options to choose from and I tried several. I even attempted using a marriage site but I certainly was not ready for that. I will say, the algorithms that some of those websites use are way off. With unlikely matches and pairing you with people that you are not attracted to whatsoever. The list could go on and on. I even attempted using paid websites and what happened there was equally disappointing. Trying to find a soul mate or your spouse through a website is something that seems completely foreign to me.

What happened through my grand experiment with dating websites? I did finally meet someone that I was physically attracted to and her I. We met on a free "Christian" dating website. She lived quite a ways from me but with the lack of success that I was having, I drove to her town to meet her. We quickly fell into a relationship at least in the sexual sense.

I took her on a trip to visit the Florida Keys over a weekend and we stayed at my sister's vacation rental. She and her family were there on vacation and it was the only chance I had to visit them. On that trip, my new girlfriend packed a large Bible but never opened it. I had many Bible teachings available to listen to on the road trip and offered that option while on the drive but she did not want to hear any of it. I thought that was strange but here we were traveling together.

After that trip, we were only able to see each other on the weekends because of the distance; my work schedule, and she did not have a vehicle at the time. The arrangement of sexual encounters and many hours of driving back and forth did not last long. We did go on some dates, dining out but that just did not feel like a relationship.

The breaking point came about one month into our relationship when we were on the phone and she asked me to pay her bills. I was taken aback by this. Yes, we were in an active sexual relationship but we did not know each other well. We had jumped into it as we both had strong sexual desires. Again, here I was being led by the flesh.

I explained to her, that I was barely making it on my own. I had my house, utilities, credit card bills, and two dogs to take care of. She was insulted by that and attempted to guilt me into giving her money. She even played the relationship card out fully and said "If I cared about her, I would help her out by paying her bills"

I wanted to hang up on her as she said that. I realized that she had been playing me and looking for someone to pay her way. Her mom and dad lived close by her and she had two older teenage children that lived with her. I had only met them once during our brief relationship. Strangely enough, I had met per parents the first time I came to visit her at her home.

Here I was again, as quickly as I had gotten into a relationship it ended just as quickly. I was not going to allow myself to be played like that or to be taken advantage of. There were some lessons that I learned from that short-lived relationship.

One, some women were available but were only looking for money or to be financially taken care of. Two, there are plenty of fake Christians, even though I had met the woman on a "Christian" website that meant almost nothing. I know there are men out there that fall into the same category of usury. The most important lesson that I was learning was that a sexual relationship is part of the marriage covenant, which God created.

Chapter 44 Takeaway: Unequally Yoked

My flesh was still leading me in my search for someone special. When looking for a spouse, you do not want to be unequally yoked.
How do you let God lead you and not your flesh?

Bible verses to reflect upon:
Psalms 62:5
2 Corinthians 6:14

Chapter 45

Dreams and Visions

It seems that I had gotten off track in my search for connecting with God. I had one failed relationship after another and one unsuccessful date after another. What was going on with me?

I had fallen back into and was still being driven by the flesh. In September 2012 one day after work, I was driving home listening to my personal mix of music on my stereo. Three songs played on shuffle mode that just shook me to my core. They each spoke to me about my life, my music, and what was I doing? That night when I went to sleep, God spoke to me. Not in a verbal voice but through three powerful dreams that came one right after the other. Here is what happened.

I was on an elevated walkway, walking on top of a cage. It was a large area that was inside of a massive structure. What I walked up to and witnessed was a large white Bengal tiger that was clinging to the floor grate beneath my feet. Her claws were bloody and she growled a loud growl but had a look of sadness on her face. Below her on the far side of that space was a large red dragon that had thin lines of yellow color running along its body. That was a disturbing scene and it made me feel sad, as the tiger was trapped and wanted out, it wanted to be set free.

The scene changed and I was now outside on a winding concrete sidewalk. There were trees and green grass. It was sunny but shaded with all the trees. It felt like spring or early summer. There were many men dressed in robes, which all seemed to be the same tan color. Then there was one man dressed in white with a stole draped over his shoulders, as you would see at a graduation ceremony.

These men were all in a line, slowing moving forward and the man in white was putting neck ribbons on each one of them. I was off slightly in the distance observing everything and no one interacted with me, as no one knew I was there.

The third and final scene that happened took place in a city at night. It was on an ice skating rink that was well lit. There were tall buildings of various shapes and sizes. I could see the mountains in the near distance. As I was skating a slender woman dressed in white with long brunette hair came up beside me. She took my left hand and proceeded to lead the way as I skated with her. I was just behind her, not beside her. She had on a white winter coat and white hat with a pom-pom top to it. As she led me in skating I looked up to see the mountain skyline and a clock tower in one of the buildings.

I woke up and decided that I needed to talk to someone about all of this as soon as possible. There was only one friend at that time and I thought of her instantly. She was a woman I had met online but never dated. We became friends and we had only ever messaged each other and texted. I reached out to her and said that I needed to talk to her. She agreed and we had our first conversation on the phone.

She was a Pentecostal church-going woman and I still had the longhaired rocker look with hair down to my waist. I also had too many worldly things in my life including the music I was listening to, for her to consider dating me at the time. We were friends though and she had a prophetic gifting from God and would feel things in the spirit at certain times.

After I told her about the dreams in full detail, she gave me her interpretation for each sequence. I appreciated her insight and it helped me to see more clearly what God was saying to me through the dreams. The interpretations were simple enough.

The white tiger that was trapped was my artist side. Wanting to create artwork and music, being a musician and writer. The men in tan robes with a leader dressed in white represented the church. It was my longing for fellowship and to be a part of the body of Christ.

The woman at the ice skating rink was my wanting a female companion; a soul mate, a spouse and it contained the only geographical clue of the three visions. God had spoken profoundly to me through the three dreams and I was on my way!

Chapter 45 Takeaway: A Prophetic Word

Sometimes God has to get your attention while you are asleep, this happened to me.
God had been purging people out of my life to prepare me for the journey ahead.
When God speaks, do you listen?

Bible verses to reflect upon:
Psalms 139:13
John 16:13

Chapter 46

Searching

With the incredible experience and blessing that I received from God, I began to look at mountainous areas that I might want to relocate to.

I had a co-worker friend that had previously lived in Raleigh, North Carolina. He and I talked about many things and with the visions that God had given me, I talked with him and did some research on the Raleigh area. That area quickly turned out to not be the one. It just did not feel right and I had to keep looking, but where?

As a second choice, I chose Nashville, Tennessee and that too did not take long to fall apart before I could even attempt planning a trip to go visit. I was thinking in the terms of a music career and almost everyone in Nashville is trying to make it in that business somehow. My search continued.

One day I was on a coffee break with a co-worker from the convention center. We were over at the hotel that was on our property having a coffee and tea break. That particular friend was only one of two that knew what was going on with me. I had given him full disclosure, as he was my best friend at work. We were talking about where I might go after Raleigh and Nashville both did not feel like the right move and they were now off the table. It was just him and I, as the hotel bar and restaurant were empty that day.

Someone spoke to me and it was not my friend drinking tea. The voice said, "Look at Denver." Puzzled, I looked around to see where the voice had come from and no one was there. My friend did not hear the voice and Denver had not even been on my radar at that point. I finished my workday and headed home to start researching Denver, Colorado.

It did not take long for things to come into focus with that location. I had found a great statistical website when I was looking at the other two geographical locations previously. It had every statistic that you could want for every city in the United States; however, the most important factor was that it felt right.

I wasted little time in starting to plan a trip. Work was busy and I knew that I would have to choose carefully about when to go to Denver. I decided to go shortly before Thanksgiving, as I wanted to have business days to perhaps find a place to live and look for work. I had to discuss it with my manager and I told him that I had family out that way, which was true. I was responsible for our work crew's schedule and we had a weekly event meeting each Wednesday. I planned to fly out around those two things.

My friend who helped me with the paperwork for my divorce years earlier had agreed to take me to and from the airport in Tampa. I had a neighbor lady that was in her seventies whom I had become friends with after her husband died. She was more than happy to take care of my two dogs, Roscoe and Baley.

I felt God was calling me out of Florida because before the three-dream night, I felt like I was dying there, at least spiritually speaking. I was ready to go and explore Denver, Colorado and see what it was that God had for me and was calling me to.

Chapter 46 Takeaway: God's Messenger

God had my undivided attention and I was searching for where to go.
I was not looking at the right place and He spoke to me where I was to go.
Has God given you direction and have you listened?

Bible verses to reflect upon:
Proverbs 8:34
John 15:14-16

Chapter 47

Denver

My trip was a five-day vacation. I flew to Denver on a Wednesday evening and would spend Thursday, Friday, Saturday, and most of Sunday there before flying back to Tampa on Sunday night.

When I landed at Denver International Airport, or simply DIA it was dark. The airport was in the middle of nowhere, miles from the city. I guess they expected massive growth as they put the airport on thousands of acres of farmland. Thankfully, I had a rental car and hotel already arranged as I had purchased a travel package. I quickly did an upgrade on my automobile though as the car they had chosen to give me was on the tiny side. I made it to the hotel, which was not far from the airport, and settled in to go to bed. It was raining and cold when I arrived in Denver that night.

When I awoke the next morning, I opened the curtains and to my surprise, I could not see the Rocky Mountains. I knew I was only about fifteen miles from the city of Denver and thought, where are the mountains? I took a closer look at the skyline and there was fog that had rolled in from last night's cold, rainy weather. I had an Atlas map book of the United States and opened it up to take a look at the surrounding area.

I left the hotel and headed west to where the mountains were. I had to travel into Denver before I could see the mountains because it was just that foggy. As I was driving along Interstate 70, it appeared to me that I might not be able to explore the mountains unless I chose an exit. As the interstate was winding through the northern part of the city and headed towards the mountains, I saw a sign for State Route 40. I chose that exit simply because there is a state route in Florida that runs north and south called State Route 41. It is a beautiful scenic route that you can take instead of interstate travel and I thought that I might find the same kind of beauty on that route too.

I came to an intersection at the bottom of the hill; there was a coffee shop and a gas station. I chose to go into the coffee shop and ask what was around as I was from out of town. The shopkeeper told me that Wild Bill's final resting place and homestead was just up the hill a little way. She also said that the Cabrini Shrine was up there as well.

I thought I would go explore where those locations were up the hillside road. As I drove along the state route I could see the interstate below me. The road curved up the hillside and I was taken back by the beauty of the evergreens, mountains, and the light snow covering. I stopped and took some photos with my camera and then continued going upward on the hillside road.

I passed some signage on the right side of the road but could not see what it said. I then looked in the rearview mirror and saw a large white image on top of the mountain. It was now behind me and I had the thought, how did I miss that? I turned around and drove slowly back in the other direction. I was able to see the sign now and it said "Mother Cabrini Shrine" as I turned in.

The road was cut into the hillside and zigzagged up until it leveled out towards the top of the hill. I drove up to the church and stopped. There was a gift shop there, so I went in to ask about the property. I talked with the manager and she explained the history of the property and what all was there on the grounds. I asked about the statue that I had seen from the road. She explained to me how to get there; to just go down the other hill and that there were a hundred and fifty steps that would take me up to where the statue was located. I followed her directions and saw the prayer chapel and garden area along the way. When I reached the beginning of the steps, there was a sign that cautioned me about snow and ice being present.

I proceeded to climb the steps and only laughed at the little warning sign about ice. As I went along there were many beautiful portraits along the way. These were the Stations of the Cross. It was a long way to the top as the steps turned and there were several landings. The temperature was dropping and the wind was picking up. Then there were pockets of snow and ice, just as the little sign had said.

Once I made it to the top, several features were stunning. Some stones had been carved out in pictures and paintings of The Ten Commandments. Each commandment had its own stone and there was a protective covering over the carved and painted area of each stone. There was the twenty-two-foot-tall white and gray statue of Jesus Christ that I had seen from the road. It was cold and windy that morning and I had worn the heaviest coat that I owned. I had not noticed but there was a young couple that came up behind me. I presumed they were tourists as they were underdressed for the weather. They did not stay long but quickly looked around and then ran back down the steps to the parking lot.

What happened next is just about beyond words. There I stood on a mountaintop outside of Denver with a large statue of Jesus Christ. The Lord came down and encompassed the entire area where I was standing. It was like the atmosphere changed and became dense. There was a heavy, weighty presence that felt huge to me. I knew with every fiber of my being that God was there with me. Not an angel but God, The Almighty, the Alpha, and the Omega, the beginning and the end. I was overcome and could not speak; I took a knee and bowed down in front of the statue, the image of God, our Lord Jesus Christ.

I dedicated myself to Him at that moment and said that I will go to wherever you are calling me. I had never felt anything like His presence ever before. After His presence lifted, I gathered my thoughts and headed down the steps to the parking lot. On the morning of the first day, the first place that I was led to was a mountaintop experience with God. I knew without a doubt that I was in the right place.

Chapter 47 Takeaway: Mountaintop Meeting

I had made the trip but was not sure what would happen once I got there.
God guided my steps and led me to meet with Him.
Has God called you and have you answered Him?

Bible verses to reflect upon:
1 Samuel 15:22
John 15:1-5

Chapter 48

Colorado Calling

I was beyond amazed by what God had done. I had been seeking Him whole heartily for nearly the last four years. He sent a messenger to speak to me about traveling to Denver. Once I arrived there, He drew me to a mountaintop. He came down and met with me there, where He was welcomed, loved, and revered. I had no idea what else I would find in the coming days but one thing was for certain. God had called me to Colorado. I finished my vacation by exploring the Denver area and God guided me to the neighborhood that I would eventually live in months later.

I looked for work and handed out many resumes throughout the audiovisual employers that I could find. I even had an interview while on vacation; I did not end up working for them later but it was still nice to be considered for a position. It was almost time for me to head back to Florida. Before I left though, I drove back out to the mountain on Sunday morning where God had met me. I was at peace and was going to have much work to do in the coming months to move to Denver.

When I returned home I chose to keep my special visit with God to myself. I started to secretly plan my departure from the state of Florida. My two closest friends at work and my Pentecostal friend who lived ninety minutes away knew the day would come for me to leave but no one else.

My manager who had been in place since May 2007 was a different kind of man. He was bipolar and was not on medicine at the time. We did not have the best relationship as he was somewhat disrespectful to me often and my work friends had taken notice. It was for that reason alone, that I kept my departure a close secret.

I began to work on the house in an attempt to sell the property. Work began immediately after I returned home. Something else happened after my vacation, something I had been praying about for a long time.

One day I was in my office and had planned to go to the local Target store to pick up an item that only they had in stock. As I sat there working, I kept hearing "go to south Target". I heard it over and over again. The city was just large enough that they had two of almost everything for retail stores. The city had a north side and a south side where the stores were predominately located. I listened to the voice, as it seemed like the same voice that had instructed me to look at Denver. I left on my lunch break and went to the south store as instructed. I had the item that I was looking for in hand and as I was walking towards the front of the store, someone caught my attention.

She was across the store a long way from me down an aisle but I walked towards her. Much to my surprise, it was my ex-wife. We had not seen each other since our divorce was finalized; it had been over five years ago. As I approached her, I simply said to her "hey stranger!" She was nervous at first but I had a smile on my face and calm energy or a sense of peace about me, as I was happy to see her. So she relaxed as we began to talk.

We had been best friends for three years, then married and divorced in a total of seven months. It had been an abrupt ending to a relationship that meant the world to me at the time. Through the pain and there was much of it that I had to work through, I began to ask God for closure. In the last couple of years, I had been asking that I could meet with her. I just wanted one last meeting to talk for a moment and have closure with our relationship.

Now, here we were in the middle of a retail store with both of us on our lunch breaks from work. We were having the conversation I had been asking God for. We talked for about forty-five minutes and the time flew by. We talked about her leaving and quickly caught up about the last five years. We both then realized that we should get going. I looked at her and I asked if we could have a simple hug. She agreed, we hugged and went our separate ways. No phone number exchange or anything like that. It was closure and goodbye for me. I did not share any of the information about my leaving or my Colorado trip. God had heard my prayers for the last several years and I had grown enough that He answered my prayer that day.

Chapter 48 Takeaway: Closure

I had asked for closure for several years and it was given to me after growing and maturing through seeking God.
Have you ever had a prayer that was delayed but revealed the need for growth?

Bible verses to reflect upon:
Isaiah 43:18-19
Hebrews 10:23

Chapter 49

Distractions

Before my trip to Colorado, I had been somewhat focused on physical exercise and trying to add muscle. I had been working out for years, on-again, off-again and not ever sticking with it. I had been committed but had reached a plateau in my lifting.

My friend from work, who had lived in Raleigh, was a dedicated weight lifter. He helped me out with tips, exercises, and workout suggestions. We never did work out together; as I had a fair amount of equipment at home and he had a gym membership where he lived. He had been lifting weights for years and it was part of a daily routine for him. In addition to exercise tips and suggestions, he gave me his input on pre-workout and post-workout drinks for me to add to my routine.

As someone who had previous addictions, I found that some of those pre-workout drinks were just too much. When I shared with my friend that this was not working, he suggested that I would have to look to steroids to get past my plateau. That was it for me; I was done. I was not going to go down the road of steroids.

After that conversation, I turned my attention to a fitness community-style website. There were free exercises you could do by watching recorded videos. There were also dozens of trainers available if you purchased a program. I should not have been surprised by what happened next.

I met a woman on the fitness and exercise website that had her own fitness studio. She was active on the website, promoting her business and Facebook page. She was beautiful and extremely fit. It started out simply enough, by me asking fitness questions. I had no idea where the friendship would eventually lead me.

Our friendship had developed initially through those fitness discussions. She had previously been overweight and was married with two children. Something had happened with her where she was no longer happy with her size. Then she found fitness and became a fanatic with it. She was a bikini fitness competitor and shared many pictures on social media.

We were only friends and then one day there was a shift. We exchanged phone numbers and we started texting each other. That was several months into our friendship. She lived in another state and was about four hundred miles from me. Most importantly though, she was still a married woman.

Early one morning I woke up and she had texted me something I was not expecting. It was a partially nude photo of herself that she had taken. I did not know how to respond to the text and photo. I was attracted to her but what about her husband? What was going on in her marriage? It was odd that she had done that because I had not asked for such a photo at any time. When I asked her about it and why she sent it. She made light of it and the situation that she had just created. She said she was just feeling sexy and wanted to show me.

Before this, we had never had a phone call and there was a good reason for that. I soon found out that she had traded her food addiction for exercising and sex addictions. When we finally talked on the phone that is what she said to me. I chose to pause the friendship, as I felt conviction from God about what she had done and what her motives might have been.

Around that time I was also feeling the draw to get closer with God on a personal level. I felt like I should go to church for Easter. It was early that year and fell on March 31st. I only had one friend that went to church and thought I would feel comfortable going with. I reached out to my Pentecostal friend and asked her. She was surprised by the request but welcomed the idea, it was not a date but church. We would go to church together and then have fellowship over lunch.

I continued to work on my housing projects in the hopes that I could sell the home and finance my move across the country. God was working things out in my life and guiding my steps towards my exit.

Chapter 49 Takeaway: Stay Focused

I knew that God wanted me to relocate to Denver.
I was struggling with my flesh and had almost put myself in a dangerous relationship.
How do you keep your flesh under control and in check?

Bible verses to reflect upon:
Proverbs 7:24-27
Colossians 2:8

Chapter 50

Pentecost

The day had finally come and I drove over to meet her and her daughter for church. We had been friends for over two years and had never met until that moment.

I had not set foot in a church in decades. I had my falling out at age fourteen and only went to church until age eighteen to appease my parents back then. This was something different though, I wanted to go to church and I had grown closer to God.

Now I had never been to a Pentecostal church and I did not know at the time what it even meant to be a Pentecostal. My friend had been in the church for over a decade herself and raised her daughter, who was seven at the time in that church. It was a small church with pews but everyone I met that day was sincere.

We sat in her pew and sat far enough apart to be appropriate for the setting. I do not recall the message, as there was an elderly gentleman who sat next to me. My friend told me he was ninety-eight years old. It was not so much his age but what he said during the service. He was speaking in tongues, almost the entire service. I was not sure what I was hearing but it sounded ancient. I thought it was Hebrew and it may have been.

The music was different than anything I had ever heard at any church I had gone to before. The music was upbeat and they were all into what they were playing and singing. Those people were passionate about God and how they worshiped Him.

I know it was Easter and that the resurrection message was preached. The pastor was fired up and passionate about the message and it came through in his preaching. He moved around on the small platform, as he did not just stand behind the pulpit for the entire message.

I met a few people including the pastor after service. He was glad that I came to church that day. I met a couple of the musicians as well. Everyone that I met was so nice, had a smile on their face, and welcomed me in. I did not feel that anyone was judging me for my long hair, as it was pulled back and I was dressed in some of my nicest clothes.

After church, we went to a local restaurant that my friend liked. She and her daughter sat across from me and we talked about life. I shared with her how things were going with my planning to move and she talked about her work and home life. It was a nice ending to a beautiful day. I then headed out for my nearly ninety-minute commute home. What happened on that Easter Sunday would be the beginning of an incredibly special walk for me that would take me to the truth I was looking for.

Chapter 50 Takeaway: First Pentecostal Church

I had felt the draw for going to church on Easter Sunday; it was my first Pentecostal service.

I did not know how God was preparing me before moving across the country.

Do you trust God with the big details in your life?

Bible verses to reflect upon:
1 Kings 8:56
Ephesians 2:20-22

Chapter 51

Repairs and Restoration

There was much going on with working my full-time job and trying to make my house as nice as it could be for a possible sale in Florida.

My home was a doublewide mobile home and when it was built, they had installed wallpaper panel boards. They were drywall boards but they had patterns on them, just like wallpaper. Attempting to peel these coverings off was a completely fruitless effort. I talked to my neighbor who was a professional painter and he informed me, the only thing that covers them that allows you to paint was a product called Killz. I mention it because it was an oil-based primer that only comes in white. Once you have primed the surface, then you can paint it. In some of the areas, I had to apply two coats of primer and then two coats of paint. As you can imagine I spent a great deal of time painting with that process.

There were many things that I had done to improve the home since my divorce. Over the last five-year period, I had completed painting of the interior and exterior. I remodeled the guest and master bathrooms. Mostly cosmetic things but I had installed real sinks, replacing the original plastic ones in each bathroom.

My friend and I had rebuilt the sun deck and I had added a row of privacy fencing to the back property line with a contractor. I later hired my weight lifting friend and his contractor to put another row of privacy fence up on one side. That gave the yard a long L-shaped privacy fence to go along with the sun deck. My friend and neighbor, the painter then stained all of this wood with his professional sprayer. Everything looked absolutely beautiful.

The day finally came for me to have a realtor come out and look the place over to see what we could list it for. The first realtor was a man and he was a shrewd businessman if he was anything at all. He advised me, that I would have to sell at a loss. His reasoning was that because I owed more than it was currently worth.

The housing market had gone through a terrible crash in 2008. The news had been reporting during President Obama's second term that the recession was over. The news media never came to central Florida. We were still in the recession and although it is true that the coastlines of the state had recovered from the recession the rest of the state had not.

I rejected the first realtor's advice and consulted with a second. She was a much nicer realtor but offered me the same outcome. She did suggest that I could attempt to sell the house on my own or turn it into a rental property. She offered her services as a property manager if I chose to go into the rental market.

With that new information, I set out on my own and chose to do a For Sale By Owner listing. That turned out to be a non-starter. I was not asking for an outrageous amount of money but the listing generated zero interest. It was not the outcome I was hoping for. I believe I gave it about thirty days on the market and I even lowered the price. As much as I had been praying about things and had a timeline for myself to exit the state of Florida, I was moving faster than God was on the move.

I was faced with the realization that I would have to turn my home into a rental property. I contacted the female realtor who had offered her services as a property manager. She came back out to the house and did a full inspection with me. There were a few small things that I had to do but the house was in great shape as I had just tried to sell it on my own.

I would have to rethink my finances and how I was going to do the move. When was I going to give notice and leave my job with the city? I would have to sit down with someone from the retirement department and start to formulate a new financial plan. God was working things out on His timeline and I would have to adjust mine to His.

Chapter 51 Takeaway: God's Timing

I was working hard on trying to accelerate my departure from Florida.
Sometimes we can get in a hurry and want to rush things; God's timing is right on time.
Have you had to learn to wait on God and His timing?

Bible verses to reflect upon:
Psalms 37:7-9
Luke 12:36

Chapter 52

Loneliness of Heart and Waiting

I had developed a friendship with yet another woman at work. It just kind of happened as we were attracted to each other and there was friendly flirting between us. I knew I was leaving in a few months as I had planned for a summer departure, since I was moving to a cold-weather state and I was ready to get out of Florida.

It was not easy to keep myself in check with another possible relationship with yet another woman co-worker. I could not explain to her what I was planning on doing, so I had to keep my distance and we only ever texted with each other. That was tempting enough to want to go out with her. However, I could not do that to her or myself, as it would not be fair to either one of us.

Just as I thought that I had that situation under control, the fitness woman from another state reappeared in my life. We started texting again and talked a couple of times. The last conversation that I had with her was about my planning my trip to move across the country to Colorado. She revealed to me that she and her husband were not on good terms and asked if I would come through her town on my journey. Red flags continued to jump out at me and I explained to her that I was not sure just what route I would take. It was in that conversation that I realized she wanted to have a fling with me if I would only come through her area to visit.

I had also learned that her husband was a police officer and that just added another red flag in addition to the first of her being married. I thought "no thank you" as I had no desire to be a home wrecker or to possibly get shot in the process. Our communications did not cease completely but slowed way down after this. I did not need that kind of drama in my life.

I turned my focus to the financial aspect of my exit and started to make a plan. I had made a friend at the financial division of work about a year earlier. I had worked part-time for almost three years before being promoted and had money in a fund that I could borrow from. Once I went full-time, I then had a pension with the city. She had helped me borrow money from the part-time account for a down payment on an automobile previously and that is how I had gotten to know someone in the department.

She was well versed in finance and I decided to make an appointment with her to plan out my retirement and exit. The finance department was like Human Resources, so I was able to give her full disclosure of when I wanted to leave and look at my part-time retirement account as well as my pension account. She helped me look at both accounts and I would have to repay the money that I had previously borrowed in the process of closing those accounts and moving the money. I had to choose when my last day of work would be and then there would be a paperwork shuffle that would set everything into motion. That had to be precise and I did have a date picked out.

Although once again, I was moving too fast and God had to correct me with His timeline. One day, I was outside of the arena on a call with my mother. I would step outside for privacy reasons and on that day my manager was being unkind to me once again. I was ready to give my notice; I had had enough of him and the disrespect he had shown me too many times. I was going to do it.

As I took a step towards the employee entrance door I felt a giant hand press against my chest and heard "not yet" in the spirit. I am not sure who that very large angel was but his hand was the size of my chest. I took heed, told my mom what had just happened as I was still on the phone with her and she said, "God is telling you it's not quite time yet." I had to gather my thoughts and go back inside to finish my workday. I would have to pray about the timeline and meet with my financial friend again.

Chapter 52 Takeaway: Do Not Hurry

My housing situation was being worked out with my realtor but I had another problem. I was ready to quit my job and God delayed me for His timing.
When you can see the promises ahead, how do you wait on God?

Bible verses to reflect upon:
Isaiah 55:8-9
1 John 2:17

_____
_____
_____
_____
_____
_____
_____
_____
_____
_____
_____
_____

Chapter 53

Television Ministries

In addition to the program I watched each morning before work, I had a couple of others that I became students under. I discovered another teacher who sat at a table and read the Word as plainly as having a conversation with someone. He was down to earth and spoke like a friend would to you. I enjoyed his plain and simplified style of teaching. There was a fireplace with a view of the Rocky Mountains behind him and he was based in Colorado.

I had also found a local preacher that was on Sunday nights. The man taught the Bible but also talked about politics and what was wrong with leadership in our country. That was refreshing, as I had never heard any preacher come out against politicians like that before. I started watching him each Sunday night and one service he invited anyone that needed healing to come to church the following Sunday. I had decided that I would go as I had sustained injuries to my back a couple of times from other people hitting my automobile from behind.

There is something that I must share with you that happened before I went to his church. I had pictures from my female fitness friend that I had downloaded of her from social media in addition to the nude photo of herself that she had sent me. In the flesh, I would have liked to have been with her but in the spirit and my heart, I knew it was wrong and could not be.

I had stopped looking at pornography but had this attraction to her. That was the last time I engaged in self-gratification and I felt terrible immediately after. There was a shift in my spirit that day and I felt it. I was done with that kind of behavior and that addiction.

The Sunday came for me to go to the healing service at his church. It was exactly sixty-eight miles one way over to the Gulf side of the state to Tarpon Springs. I was not sure what would happen that day but I was open to God moving and having His way in the service. As I walked in, there were two large television cameras, the stage, the pulpit, and plenty of seating. I went down towards the front and sat a few rows back. He came out and welcomed everyone and advised us on how things were going to be done. It was Sunday morning service, they would record and then we would have the healing service followed by a luncheon.

The praise and worship team, led by his daughter came out and performed a couple of songs. Then He came and preached the message and they stopped filming. He then announced that anyone that had come for healing should come down to the front alter area of the church. I got up from my seat, walked down to the front, and stood to the right of the podium fairly close to the stage. He proceeded to say that he was going to pray over us then he was going to speak to the demons that were in the room with us. I was taken back by what he just said but was willing to receive prayer.

He prayed over us and then went right into prayer against the demons that were there that day. He invoked the name of Jesus and spoke on the authority of His Word and commanded the demons that were there to come out! In the name of Jesus and he cast them into outer darkness. He commanded them to leave the planet and to go into outer space and to not return in the name of Jesus.

As he was speaking the command for them to come out, the strangest thing happened to me. I began to feel a churning and burning in my lower left abdomen area just above my pelvic region. It felt like something was being unscrewed, loosened from within me. It burned and then it left and was gone. What just happened to me? I had been set free!

I had carried a demonic spirit inside of my physical body for many years, maybe decades, as my first exposure to pornography went back to age nine. I had been unaware of the possibility until recent years as I studied God's Word and the ministry of Jesus

Christ. In His ministry here on earth, in almost every encounter with sick or oppressed people Jesus cast out demons.

I cannot say for certain when that demon entered my body and had influence over my sexual desires and lusting in the flesh. My first thought is at age thirteen as I was entering puberty and there had been sexual confusion in my life. But God, on that day, set me free! Because I was willing to receive and believe in Him, I was now on my way to a better life with Him!

We had a wonderful luncheon afterward and I got to meet the pastor, his wife, and a few people. He also had on the property a large Bible collection in display cases. He had various translations and had one Geneva Bible from 1583. It was truly a great day and I felt so much better and completely different than I had when the day started. Praise God for his goodness and mercy!

Chapter 53 Takeaway: Follow His Lead

I believe God led me to this church that taught directly from the Bible.
I had my own first-hand experience of the power of Jesus' name when used properly.
Have you had addictions that you had a great struggle breaking free from?

Bible verses to reflect upon:
Psalms 31:3
Mark 16:7

Chapter 54

Being Set Free

That wonderful event happened on May 5, 2013. It was a personal and private experience and at the time, I only shared it with my mother. She and I were close but I think it came as a surprise to her, that her son had carried a demonic spirit with him for all those years.

I will say that it felt like a small entity but what you have to understand is the following; those spirits have some influence over your thoughts. You are still in control of your own body but it is the thought process that is hindered. I had wanted to stop looking at pornography and engaging in self-gratification for many months as I grew closer to the Lord.

Why did I keep slipping? I would engage in that destructive behavior, then feel terrible and ask for forgiveness. I even confessed to God, that I did not want to do it again. It would not be until a little while later, that the full explanation would be revealed to me.

The answer would come through another television preacher who is an incredible teacher. He explained that particular addiction in great detail, almost word for word, what I had struggled with in that season of my life. He said, "You're dealing with a demon" while explaining the destructive behavior and repetitive cycle that I had gone through with pornography.

He too, as a young man had a looking, lusting, and sexual addiction problem that he had to overcome. That was the confirming answer that I had been looking for. After being set free, I was completely focused on my timeline to exit my job and collect the money that I had in retirement. God had revealed to me that was how He would finance my move of almost two thousand miles across the country.

My financial friend had tried to talk me into rolling my pension over into another account and saving it. The part-time retirement account had a few thousand dollars in it but that was not going to be enough money. I politely informed her that I needed all of my money from the city, both from the part-time retirement fund and my full pension.

Those were all going to be paper checks and they had different dispersal dates. I had finally selected the date for my leaving my job. My last day of work would be Saturday, June 1st. The pay period ended that day and we were paid bi-weekly. I had the calculated dates from the finance department for the checks I would be receiving. I had planned to leave Florida by July 1st.

One of the last things that I had to do was give notice to my manager. I had already written my resignation letter and merely had to change the date on it. I remember that day like it was yesterday. My manager and I, most days just did not have a good relationship as he was bipolar and not on medication. We had worked together five years and it was not all bad or I would have left sooner.

When I asked if we could talk, he had me wait a few minutes, as he was busy. When I handed him the letter and sat down on the couch in his office, he read it and then looked at me and said, "Is this real?" When I said, "Yes, I am moving to Colorado to be closer to my family" his hand started to shake and he got up and left. He did say that he would be right back and to wait for him. He went over to talk with upper management and inform them that I had just resigned.

The next couple of weeks were awkward for me. He made off-handed comments like "you sure kept that a secret". There was a good reason for that and I only wanted to give him the two weeks' notice because of those reasons. He did ask for my thoughts on my replacement and there were only two men on the crew that could possibly step in at the time. The department and our location had gone through an exodus of sorts with many people leaving. The replacement was chosen and I was tasked with training him on how I did my job. It went fairly well as my replacement was one of our full-time technicians and we worked together daily already.

Working for the city at a specific location as I did, the news spread like wildfire. I had been there nine and a half years and knew many people. My manager and my closest friends gave me a farewell dinner at a local restaurant. It was a bittersweet moment for me as some of those people were real friends. My second friend at work whom I had many talks with was the Sales Manager. She was such a nice lady who was a flower child at heart. She and her husband opened up their home and had a going-away gathering for me as well.

There were people from work that had previously retired and a few of the same friends from the restaurant gathering that came out again. I was truly blessed that I had people that did care and wanted me to succeed in leaving the city and moving across the country. Before those gatherings, I felt like I only had my two friends that I had confided in. I was wrong about that and it touched my heart in a special way. I was thankful for a pretty smooth exit and God's grace.

Chapter 54 Takeaway: Biblical Truth

I was set free from a demonic stronghold in my life and had received confirmation.
Jesus' name has all power when used properly with and under authority.
Do you need to be set free?

Bible verses to reflect upon:
Isaiah 8:19-20
James 4:7-8

_____
_____
_____
_____
_____
_____
_____
_____
_____
_____
_____
_____

Chapter 55

Stress and Reservations

My Sales Manager friend had offered me some advice just weeks prior as I had something rather stressful happen to me. It was in late April as I was working my full-time job, trying to find employment and a place to live in Denver, and still living in Florida. I was under a great deal of stress with my house not selling, trying to figure out the local rental market, and making plans for the move to Denver.

One day I woke up and had tiny red blisters and a rash that streaked around from my back to my stomach on my right side. It was painful and itchy, so I went to see a doctor. My doctor had recently retired, so I had to go to one of those Urgent Care places. He was a nice doctor but quick and to the point. He took one look at me and said, "You have shingles." He then asked me a couple of questions. One was, "You had chickenpox as a child, correct?" and the other was "Do you have stress in your life?" The answer to both questions was "Yes." He prescribed two medicines, one for the rash and mild pain medicine to help me sleep at night.

When I shared this news with her at work, she spoke to me quite plainly. She said God has called you to Colorado and you are going. You have money from your retirement funds, so just go. I looked at her slightly puzzled and she said it again, just go! Pack up your things, drive across the country with your dogs and just go! You will find a place to live when you get out there and you'll find work too! That was like an older sister or best friend giving me the best advice that I could have been given at that time, just go! Let the stress go, trust God and just go!

I was refreshed after that conversation with her and proceeded to plan accordingly for the move across country. There were many moving parts or puzzle pieces that did have to be put into place for the move to be set into motion. It is a large task to plan a move of two thousand miles. I had begun the packing process and giving things away. Denver was much more expensive than central Florida. I knew that from looking at rental listings while on my trip. I owned a three-bedroom home with a carpeted and air-conditioned storage building. I realized I had accumulated way too many belongings over the five-plus years since my divorce.

I found a large church that had a thrift store, a women's shelter thrift store, and other charitable places to give specific items to. I gave away many items and felt blessed to do so. It was good to downsize and I was even able to bless my neighbor, the painter with some outdoor equipment and yard items that I felt I no longer needed.

My Sales Manager friend purchased one of my nice couches and got to see my home with her husband. We had a nice visit and they went on their way. I had attempted to sell a fair amount of furniture and wound up giving away most of it to a charity that came out with a truck and hauled it away.

I reserved a truck after much shopping around; it was not just about price but the quality and maintenance of their equipment. I also opted for a car carrier that would have my newer vehicle completely off the ground to tow behind the large truck. Other than acquiring the rental equipment, I chose to hire two moving helpers to help me pack the truck. That would be done on Saturday, June 29th as I planned to leave the state on Sunday, June 30th.

Things were finally coming together although my house was a wreck most days. In between all of my packing, sorting, and giving away items, I had no one to assist me except one day my coffee friend from work came out and he helped me do some packing. Otherwise, it was just myself packing and my two dogs watching.

At one point I went back to work to visit with a few people and drop off an assortment of paints and cleaning supplies to the engineering department. When I had worked as a part-time technician, the manager of engineering hired me as a painter during our slow season. That was truly a blessing and he was a very nice man, who I considered a friend. I was able to freely donate to his department and say goodbye to him. My time was almost at hand to head out on the journey that God had set before me.

Chapter 55 Takeaway: Saying Goodbye

Things were in full motion at that time with all the preparations being made.
I had learned another lesson of not trusting in all my own abilities but to trust God.
Do you trust God for daily guidance?

Bible verses to reflect upon:
Psalms 118:8
Matthew 6:26

Chapter 56

God's Direction

In June, I went back to see the Pastor in Tarpon Springs, to say goodbye and take some photos of his rather extensive Bible collection. It was a wonderful service, luncheon, and time of visiting.

I had made plans to have dinner late that afternoon with my weight lifter friend, his girlfriend, and another friend and her husband from work. We had a nice time together and took some photographs out on the deck at the restaurant. It was truly a blessed and great day.

I then went home did some more packing and proceeded to unwind for the evening and go to bed. That day will always be remembered as one that stands out to me, it was Sunday, June 16th, which was also Father's Day. What happened next was beyond amazing.

I went to bed around 10 PM and was awakened at 11 PM. I say awakened because I felt completely refreshed as if I had slept eight hours. I thought to myself that was weird; let me see what was on television. I had a thirty-two inch in my bedroom and a forty-two inch in my living room at the time.

I sat up, turned on the television, and went to one of the Christian channels that I watched. There on the screen was a man sitting behind a desk, dressed in a tan suit. He was speaking, as I had never heard anyone speak before. He was talking about end-time events and Bible prophecy. He spoke about where we had been, where we were at, and where we were going and tied all of it in with the Bible.

The man had my full attention. I got up to go into the living room to watch him on the bigger television. I was intrigued and got my computer out to look up the channel programming. I did not have cable at the time and was using an aerial antenna for viewing. I found their website, found the listing, and then looked him up.

The program was called End of the Age and the man was Irvin Baxter. As I was looking at his website and the top of it, there were tabs for various things. There was one that said Conferences and Schedules. I clicked on it and there was a list of conferences that were occurring that summer. I looked down the list and saw Denver, Colorado for July 13th and 14th.

I immediately thought that was so cool, I was going to be there by then! I would go see him in person. Where in Denver, was the event going to be held? I looked at the listing and it said Landmark Tabernacle. I thought what is Landmark Tabernacle? I had to look them up and when I went to their website two things stood out to me. The first was the phrase "The Pentecostals of Denver" the second was their address.

Have you ever had a number stuck in your head and did not know why? When I had been in Denver on my trip back in November 2012 and was in my hotel room. I was looking for places to live and work and a number became stuck in my mind. It almost felt as though, it had been etched there.

When you are searching for things like housing and jobs online you need a zip code to do accurate searches. The number that was in my mind for eight months was 80227. Can you guess what the zip code of that church was? There it was on their website, their full address in the south Denver area with the zip code of 80227. How incredible was that! When I should have been asleep, God sent an angel to wake me up and show me all of those things!

You see I had fully committed to God. I was all in; I had rented the moving equipment, hired moving help, and was going to Denver without a place to live or a job to work. What God did in just a few moments, was to show me where I was going to be spiritually fed and have a church to call home. Thank you, Jesus!

Chapter 56 Takeaway: A New Church

I will say God was pleased with my commitment to go across the country simply knowing that He was calling me.
Then God chose to reveal my new church to me.
Has God given you divine direction in your life?

Bible verses to reflect upon:
Psalms 143:10
Hebrews 11:3

_____
_____
_____
_____
_____
_____
_____
_____
_____
_____
_____
_____

Chapter 57

Closing Doors

The morning after the revelation from God about the church in Denver, I could hardly wait to call my Pentecostal friend. I had to wait until she was up for work, I texted her, and then she called. I shared the whole experience with her and she was happy for me. We talked about getting together once more for church and saying goodbye. We had to plan for the next Sunday as I was planning to leave the Sunday after that. I still had much to do with continued packing and giving things away as I prepared for the big move.

The lead singer from the band I had worked for had gotten back in touch with me. The band had gone through some line-up changes but at one point had recorded an album at a local studio. I had been their soundman since 2008 but the band fell apart in late 2011. My friend was starting back up with some old and new people and asked me to be their soundman.

I took that moment to reveal to him, that I was leaving Florida and moving across the country. He had been a good friend and I enjoyed being his soundman and doing shows with the band previously for those few years. He and his wife invited me over for a farewell dinner and to just hang out one last time. It was a nice afternoon and evening but it is always hard to say goodbye.

The Sunday came for my visit with my Pentecostal friend. It was bittersweet for me, as I had gotten to know her over the last couple of years through social media and texting. We never did actually date, as I was a longhaired rocker seeking God and she was recently divorced and just not ready to date. We went to church and I was able to talk to her pastor again. I now had the information about where I was going to be attending church in Denver. When I told him the name of the church and who the pastor was, he said I was going to be in good hands, because he knew them.

His church was small and he did say, he wished I would reconsider and stay. I think he was being sincere but I told him politely that God was calling me to Colorado. We then left and did not go out to eat then, as I had too many things that I still needed to get done for the move. We went back to her place and talked for a few moments before I left and said goodbye to her and her daughter.

That just about brings my time in Florida to a close, as I was one week from heading out of the state. It was not easy to say goodbye to the friends that I had but I was looking forward to living by the mountains.

Chapter 57 Takeaway: Farewell My Friends

I was wrapping up my final goodbyes to a couple of my close friends and was prepared to begin the journey to Denver.
Do you pray for God's protection and guidance in your daily steps and travel?

Bible verses to reflect upon:
Psalms 121:8
2 Thessalonians 3:3

Chapter 58

Moving Day

My old friend from work, who had helped me write my statement for the divorce and then locate my wife when we were separated, helped me one last time. I was picking up a large truck and car carrier. The truck was roughly thirty-five feet long and the car carrier another fifteen feet in length. The near-sized rig that I would be driving was just over fifty feet in length. When he took me to pick it up, I knew I would have to park it on the road in front of the house until it was time to detach the car carrier. It had a full bench seat and it was a large truck; the storage area was twenty-six feet in length. The bench seat would turn out to be just right for the dogs and me.

The movers came later in the afternoon, as it was almost July and being summertime in central Florida. When I booked the help, I underestimated how long it would take. The moving company wanted to sell me four helpers but I had only booked two. That wound up costing me the time and money that I thought I was saving. The two men stuck it out and I paid the extra fee for the additional time and tipped them as well. We finished just before 11 PM and I went straight to bed after they left.

When I arose Sunday morning, I still had some of the kitchen and bathroom to pack up into the truck. I packed up our food and a cooler then checked the house over. My realtor had a complete set of keys to the house and storage building. We did not have a renter lined up for July but with the house in prime condition and it being empty, it would not be difficult to rent.

I had left the car carrier on the street in front of the house. It would be much easier to pull the truck around and line it up on a smooth flat surface. Thankfully my neighbor was home, and was able to assist me with the hook-up. He also had to help guide me as I drove my vehicle up onto the car carrier. The dogs were loaded into the front seat of the truck and were waiting with anticipation. We got everything in place and secure for my vehicle. I tested the turn signal and brakes and was ready to go. I gave my friend and neighbor a hug goodbye and we were on our way.

I took the long way out of Florida because I had a thought. That thought was we would drive through the panhandle as I had lived in Florida fifteen years and had never seen that part of the state. If you are not familiar with the state, to travel from Jacksonville in the northern tip of the state to Key West in the southernmost part of the state is five hundred miles. Florida is a large and long state.

We traveled the interstates; first, we were on I-75 and then I-10 to go across the state. We finally made it out of Florida and stopped in Montgomery, Alabama for our first night. We had traveled almost five hundred miles our first day and I was worn out. I know my dogs were just as tired even though they slept most of the way. My veterinarian had prescribed some medicine to help the dogs remain calm and sleep on our long journey. I only gave them medicine the first day as the Lord was guiding our journey and there was peace in the cab of our truck. We were well on our way and had successfully left the state of Florida. Thank God for traveling mercies, grace, and safety along the way!

Chapter 58 Takeaway: The Journey Begins

The packing was done and we were ready to depart on our journey. After months of planning and preparation, I felt God's peace as we left.
Have you ever had your faith stretched by God's calling?

Bible verses to reflect upon:
Psalms 91:11
John 14:31

Chapter 59

Traveling

Traveling with two dogs is kind of similar to traveling with children. So, they don't talk back but they do need bathroom breaks and to be able to stretch their legs. After the first day, which included the last little bit of packing and then driving almost five hundred miles, I was a little tired the next day. I had an ambitious travel agenda though, as I wanted to get to Colorado.

On the second day of travel, I was able to see many miraculous signs in the clouds. Those were not for me though as one was of a bearded man holding an infant. It was so clear and precise; it was for certain a sign for someone. We traveled at a northern angle through the state of Alabama and Mississippi. Some of the most beautiful hills that I had ever seen were in northern Mississippi.

We then ventured into Tennessee and through the city of Memphis. I remember quite clearly that Memphis was a tale of two cities. We came up from the south through Mississippi on a State Route 78 and made our way to Interstate 40. It was a nice drive and there were big houses like old plantations and on the way, I did see signs for Graceland. I remember the area being nice as we drove through the city and approached the river. I then started to see bars on the windows and it was obvious that particular area had less appeal than what we had just passed through.

We then prepared to cross the mighty Mississippi River. I had never seen it in person before and it was amazing and beautiful. Yes, it is a muddy river but the massive size of it was incredible. It is an extremely wide river and it seemed like a long drive, as I drove across the bridge. That was because the bridge is 3.3 miles in total length. It is long! As we crossed the bridge into Arkansas, we were now in West Memphis. We continued our travels into Little Rock and stayed at a hotel there. It was almost another five hundred mile day and I was now feeling it.

You may be wondering why I took this particular route to go to Colorado. The ministry that brought me back to God happened to be located in a small farming town named Gravette, Arkansas. When I started to plan our trip to move across the country from Florida to Colorado that was a stop that I felt had to be made.

It was fitting that we went to go visit the ministry on day three of our journey. It was an exciting moment for me. It was that program that brought God's Word to life for me. As we traveled to the small town, it was out in the middle of nowhere surrounded by farmland. Getting there was an adventure all its own. I experienced some stress while driving on the small country roads.

One area, in particular, stands out to me, as they had put a road through the solid rock side of a mountain. Where we were, there was no guardrail and we were way up in this fifty-foot truck and trailer that I was driving. That was fine until a large dump truck came our way, he was in his lane but it was still stressful, as I had to ride the edge on the small mountain road. God got us through it but it was a white-knuckle experience for me. That was on a stretch of road that was up in the Ozark Mountains.

We arrived safely and I was pleasantly surprised to find they had a large parking lot, which was nice because of the size of our truck. They had a church building and a separate gift shop and studio area for filming. They even had an area where a small audience could sit and watch the pastor do his broadcast. On the day of our visit, there was no broadcast being filmed as it was close to July 4th. There was a nice man who gave me a guided tour and I was able to see the desk and the chair, where the pastor sat. He allowed me the opportunity to sit in the chair and I politely declined and said it was just a pleasure to see it.

It was such a joy to be there, to see it in person. They have a stone and concrete sign that says, "I AM THAT I AM" out in front of their property, quoted from Exodus 3:14. The man who gave me the tour was kind enough to take my picture by the sign and I still have it to this day. I also purchased my first study Bible that has a special place in my heart from the gift shop before leaving that day.

It was a wonderful day even with a touch of stress on the drive to Gravette. It was well worth it and I am so glad that the dogs and I made the trip. I had slowed our pace down mileage-wise and was spiritually recharged at our midway point. We traveled north and went to Joplin, Missouri to rest and relax at a hotel before heading out on day four of our journey.

Chapter 59 Takeaway: Seeing the Church

We had traveled many miles and made a special stop to the ministry that had helped bring me back to God and love His Word. Do you take time to stop, reflect, and thank God along the journey?

Bible verses to reflect upon:
Psalms 100:4-5
Acts 17:26-27

Chapter 60

Almost There

We had traveled just under one thousand three hundred miles in three days. That was a long journey. You do not realize how long a thousand miles is until you start driving. Let alone almost two thousand miles across the country. My dogs were angels though; they were so well behaved and slept the many hours that I drove each day. They were just happy to be with me.

After our side trip to Gravette, Arkansas I decided to change gears and do a little sightseeing as we traveled. When we left Joplin, Missouri and instead of going north on the interstate, I went cross-country through the southern part of Kansas. We traveled State Routes until we came to Interstate 35 and then 135. We took that through Wichita, which happened to be another place that I had wanted to see, as we traveled north to interstate 70.

We then traveled across the interstate to Hays, Kansas and that was as far as I could make it and chose to call it a day. Quite a day it had been, as another long day of almost four hundred miles of driving was behind us but we were getting closer to our Denver destination. I had a nice dinner and a good rest with my dogs before the last day of our journey.

While staying at the hotel I had to do some research about our next hotel stay which would be in the Denver area. That would be our place to stay for the short term while I looked for a rental home. I had begun looking the previous night and asked God what would be our best fit.

The next morning we headed out and had our sights set on Aurora, Colorado. It is one of the largest suburbs of Denver. It is located on the east side of the city and Denver International Airport is there as well. The population of Aurora was about three hundred and thirty-two thousand at the time of our move in 2013. I felt led by God to just rest there for a short while. We arrived on July 4, 2013, and that became a special date to me now for two reasons.

The first thing that I had to do was to figure out what area I would be living in and find a storage building to put my belongings in for the time. I had the truck and car carrier rental that I would have to turn in soon. There was an area of Denver that I had felt drawn to on my trip in the fall of 2012. I decided that would be a good place to go explore.

It was incredible to see how big Denver was. It was spread out far and wide. There were some skyscrapers downtown but I would later find out most of those were bank buildings and hotels. Denver stretched from the foothills of the Rocky Mountains in the west to Aurora in the east. From Thornton in the north to Parker in the south, it was truly a massive area. God had directed my steps to bring me here and would continue to guide me in Denver. I am thankful for everything He did.

Chapter 60 Takeaway: We Arrived

God had been faithful in our journey that stretched across eight states and almost two thousand miles.
We were here, safe and sound, and thanked God!
Do you remember to thank God for the little things in life as well as the big?

Bible verses to reflect upon:
Psalms 107:8
1 Thessalonians 5:18

Chapter 61

Where Home Would Be

On a Saturday morning, I was driving out in the area that I had been led to previously and the Lord was speaking to me. Turn to the left here, turn right here, go down the street and turn left here.

Those explicit directions led me to a brick house where two men were carrying out a couch and it appeared that they were moving out. I had just turned the corner from the side street and the house was the second on the left. As I drove by and was looking I felt the need to turn around and park. On that day, the dogs were back in the hotel room as I did not know how long I would be gone or where the Lord would lead me. I loved my dogs but they would have been excited and wanted to explore parks with me. I was having some alone time with God.

As I approached the front yard, the two men looked at me rather strangely. I politely asked if the house was available, the one man said yes, the owner is inside. The other man just kind of leered at me for some reason. I walked in and was greeted by a woman, she was focused on checking the house over as we talked and walked. I informed her I was looking for a place and that it was just the two dogs and myself. She took my information and said it would be at least a couple of weeks before the house was ready to be rented out. I went on my way, feeling good about what had just transpired. I had no idea what would take place over the next several weeks.

On the first day that I went to church, I met several people, and at the time, church services were held at 10 AM and 6:30 PM. At the first service, I do not recall what was preached but I do remember going down to the altar area and that two men came to pray with me.

That was the beginning of my Pentecostal journey in Denver. When I came back for evening service, the one gentleman who prayed with me was also a greeter and welcomed me back. I again do not recall what was preached but I was making friends and was going to have some help unloading the truck the following day.

I took the car carrier back and then met three of my new friends at the storage facility that was not far from the home that God had led me to. With the four of us unloading the truck, it went by fairly quickly. Afterwards the second man who had prayed with me just the day before, gave me a ride back to the hotel in Aurora. I was so thankful for new friends and people willing to help with moving.

That same week, I was invited out to a buffet restaurant for dinner with a group of men from church. It was the men's prayer group but they were dining out and having fellowship that night. At that dinner event, I met another friend who would become one of my best friends. He worked for his brother-in-law as a maintenance man for two small apartment buildings and one unit was available. I was interested, so we went by that night to take a look after dinner.

It was small but certainly more affordable than the hotel. It was and would be a blessing! I would simply have to fill out a rental form and meet with the owner. In just a short time, things were coming together. The apartment looked like a good option because I was still waiting to hear back on the house. I was able to meet with the owner on that Saturday and finalize things for a move-in on July 15th, which was only two days away.

That was also the weekend that Irvin Baxter was at the church. He was there for a special Saturday night message and then a Sunday morning message. Between the church services and being able to secure that apartment, things were coming together for me. God was orchestrating one thing after another as I was about to get settled in Denver.

Chapter 61 Takeaway: Provision

When I was planning to leave Florida, I had wanted to move faster than God was.
His timing was just right and now He was aligning things one after another.
Do you wait on the Lord to guide and direct your steps?

Bible verses to reflect upon:
Psalms 130:5
James 1:17

Chapter 62

Irvin in Denver

I was beyond excited to be going to the large, beautiful church in Denver. In just a couple of services, I had already made a handful of friends. It was as if God was ordering my steps each day through all of my circumstances and encounters.

I had watched Irvin on television for just a short time. If you recall, I shared the miraculous story of how God showed me all of this just about a month earlier on Father's Day. Now, here I was at the church getting ready to hear Irvin Baxter preach! The pastor was on stage off to the side where there were a couple of rows of comfy chairs for preachers and guest speakers to sit.

What I remember about Saturday night's teaching was that it was long. He spoke for two hours but the time did fly by. I had never heard anyone teach or preach the way that he had that night. He covered the plan of salvation and Jesus's return to earth. He talked about the tribulation and the events written in the book of Revelation. He also talked about Satan, the false profit, the Antichrist, and the mark of the beast. Those were all subjects that you might hear one of those topics in a church service but I had never heard anyone talk about all of them in a single service.

He was passionate and he knew the book of Revelation. He talked about writing his first book back in the early 1980s and all the studying that he had done leading up to that book. He said that he had read the book of Revelation twenty-seven times during that time. I have always been intrigued by Biblical prophecy and was fascinated by the book of Revelation. It was a real joy and surreal moment for me to see him on stage doing what he did best teaching and preaching. I could not wait to come back for Sunday morning service to see and hear what he would be talking about next.

Sunday morning came and the church was almost full again, not quite as packed as Saturday night but it was still a large turnout. He talked about prophecy updates and where we were at in our present time in relation to Biblical prophecy. In both of his services, he had PowerPoint slide shows and videos of world events to show us.

I got to meet him for a moment, to say hello and that I was new to Denver and the church. He was kind and it was nice meeting him just for a moment. Many people wanted to meet him. I felt like my own prophetic vision had come to pass. What a weekend that had been! I felt like I was on cloud nine or as close to the Heavenlies as I could get. God was simply amazing and the best was still to come!

Chapter 62 Takeaway: Prophecy Fulfillment

It had been less than one month since God had shown me in one night, Irvin Baxter and my new church.
Here I was and it all came to pass. Praise God!
Has God brought a miraculous event about at any point in your life?

Bible verses to reflect upon:
Proverbs 16:20
Matthew 17:20

_____
_____
_____
_____
_____
_____
_____
_____
_____
_____
_____
_____

Chapter 63

Local Move

I had a positive attitude about everything that had happened since arriving in Denver although I had been a little worried about the hotel cost. But God quickly took care of that and put me into a nice cozy apartment. I rented a smaller truck because I was only able to put some of my things into the apartment. Which meant keeping the storage unit until I heard back about the house that I felt God would put me into soon.

My friend from church helped me out again, the man who prayed for me at my first service. It turns out he felt an instant connection with me because he too, had long hair when he came into church years before. It is important to note, that no one ever directly said anything to me during that time about my hair. Mine was very long as it came down to my waist but I always kept a clean appearance and kept it pulled back in a ponytail.

The move was quick as the nationwide company that I had rented from stuck me with an "in-town rental". I had always rented trucks for a twenty-four period and they had given me six hours. I was not pleased but my friend and I made the best of it that day. We did well with that and it was a good thing that I only had the truck for a short time. He had to go to work that afternoon and I needed to check out of the hotel with my dogs and the belongings I had there.

We finished up and made the drive from the hotel for the last time to our new place! What a day it had been already and now here we were with a mess of boxes as I had the thought of where do I begin? Before I could finish the thought, my phone rang and it was the call I had been waiting for. The property manager was on the other end and he got right to the point, as he said, "Do you still want the house?" to which I replied with an emphatic "Yes!"

He then explained to me there were quite a few repairs that still needed to be done. The previous tenant had been a smoker and most of the house was being painted on the inside. That was a blessing and worth the wait. He had called right as I was thinking about what to unpack.

That phone call made it real simple for me with unpacking things for the apartment. I would unpack only what I truly needed to get by with for a couple of weeks. He was confident that I would be in the house by the end of the month. That was fantastic news! God is so good to us when we follow after Him, when we seek Him and when we ask Him for guidance in all things!

Chapter 63 Takeaway: Taking Shape

I was learning that when God calls you to it, He will bring you through it!
We went from a hotel to an apartment to receiving the call for the house in just days!
Have you ever trusted God with something and seen Him work quickly in your favor?

Bible verses to reflect upon:
Proverbs 3:4
2 Corinthians 9:8

Chapter 64

The Next Move

The day came and it was time to sign the lease and get the keys to the house. It was on Saturday, July 27th and I would have to wait a few days until Tuesday, July 30th for moving help from my church friends.

On that day, I had two friends that stayed until the end and we then went out for dinner. One of my other friends who assisted had enough for the day and went straight home when we were done unloading. It was a long, hard day as not only did we have to empty the apartment but we also had to empty my storage unit.

Looking back at what God had done during that time and bringing all of it about is truly amazing. He called me to Denver in the fall of 2012. He brought me to that neighborhood and area on that exploration trip. Once I moved, He guided me to come over on the exact day someone was moving out. Now less than one month in Denver, I was in the house that would be my home for years to come.

That was such a blessing! There was a lake within walking distance. The neighborhood was a mix of some near historical houses and some modern construction homes. I found out that it was built in the post World War II era from 1948 to 1952. The house that I was in was a brick home, two-bedroom, and one bath. It was perfect for the dogs and me.

It took a little while to get settled in but we had moved two thousand miles and had downsized from a three-bedroom ranch home to a nice two-bedroom. The garage was long and narrow, so I put my exercise equipment out there and it worked great! It had been a long process that we had gone through. We were home and now it was time to settle in and get even more focused on God. I had time to enjoy and explore because of the money that I had from the retirement and pension funds.

It is interesting how God works and it is true that His ways are higher than ours. Sometimes we just have to trust God and take that leap of faith. I had some family members who thought I was not thinking right about doing what I had done. They just did not understand my relationship with God at the time. But God is faithful and true and is a rewarder of those who diligently seek Him.

God was about to bless me more spiritually than I could have ever imagined. I had been seeking after God diligently for years. Since I arrived in Denver a few weeks before and began attending the Pentecostal church, I was quickly becoming more rooted in God's Word. I had studied almost every day since January 2009 but had never heard anyone preach like that. God was about to show me how real He was and is!

Chapter 64 Takeaway: Our New Home

It was time to celebrate by giving God glory, praise, and thanks.
We need to remember the small things as well as the big things in life.
Have you thanked God today for the life that you are living?

Bible verses to reflect upon:
Psalms 95:1-4
Colossians 3:17

_____
_____
_____
_____
_____
_____
_____
_____
_____
_____
_____
_____

Chapter 65

Baptism

I had been sitting under the Word and the leadership of a gifted and anointed preacher. I began attending services on Sunday, July 7th. If the church was open for service, I was there. I had never in my life heard so much passion coming from behind the pulpit in church. We had church at 10 AM and 6:30 PM each Sunday and 7:30 PM every other Wednesday. On alternating Wednesdays, we had "Church in the House" or CIH for short. What was that?

Church in the house was a Bible study that was written by the pastor. Various CIH leaders would hold gatherings in their homes. There would be praise and worship songs, prayer time, lesson time, and at the end, snack time and fellowship. It was an interesting and well-thought-out program. The ultimate goal of that was to bring in neighbors and friends that were not part of the church. There were regular attendees in each neighborhood group.

While at church, several people kept asking me about baptism. They all seemed concerned that I had not been baptized in Jesus's name by water submersion. At first, I was offended by their persistence because I had been baptized as an infant. It did not take long for the Bible scriptures to sink in and hit home with me though. That was something that weighed on me and was the only part of the Pentecostal church that bothered me at that moment. The push for baptism, what was it all about, and why?

I would soon find out. In addition to services on Sunday and Wednesday, I also participated in the Men's Prayer Group on Fridays. The week of the move into my Denver home, something strange happened to me on that Friday night. Men's Prayer Group would begin with fellowship, coffee, and snacks. We would sit and talk about the week and then go into prayer requests. Once that portion was done, the group leader would turn off the overhead lights and put on praise and worship music.

We would then pray by ourselves or walk around the room and pray with one another. The room was not completely dark as there were parking lights outside the windows and ambient lighting. It set the mood though to pray in the spirit or what is called praying in tongues. This is referenced heavily in the book of Acts in the Bible. I was standing and facing a wall by the door. It was dark as usual, there was a poster in front of me that I was trying to read and focus myself to pray.

What happened next is similar to my verbal clue about looking at Denver many months prior. A voice said, "Get a haircut, Shane." I looked to my left and my right and there was no one there. No one was even close to me at the time. I leaned in and tried to focus on praying. Again, the voice said, "Get a haircut, Shane". This happened over and over and over. Many times, the voice said this to me. There was no one there. It was an angel bringing me a message that after twenty years, it was time to cut my hair. The voice did not stop until I said to him in the spirit, "All right, I will get a haircut tomorrow!"

I was not angry; I just wanted him to stop saying it. I would guess that it was perhaps ten to twelve times at the most that he said that. I did not share that with anyone. I simply went home and researched salons that I could call on Saturday morning and get my hair cut. I found a place that would take me and went in. I told the woman that I wanted to cut my hair off but make a donation to Locks of Love; they made wigs for children with cancer. She went right to it and just like that, my long hair was gone.

My first hair cut was a little rough; I believe she was trying to be kind and ease me into a shorter haircut. I went home, took pictures, and then shared with friends online what I had just done. They were shocked because I had said for many years that I would not cut my hair for any man or any job. This was different though, God was telling me to get a haircut and I did it as soon as I could the very next day. I had no idea what was going to happen next.

Chapter 65 Takeaway: Sprinkle or Submersion

My new church was showing me things that I had never known through scripture.
God was preparing me for the next big step in my walk with Him.
Has God revealed things through scripture that you thought you knew?

Bible verses to reflect upon:
Exodus 3:14
Matthew 5:8

Chapter 66

A New Me

The next day was Sunday, August 4th. One of my friends who I met while living in Aurora for the short time that I did was a minister at the church. I bumped into him at church after Sunday morning service and told him that I was thinking about getting baptized the following Sunday. He looked at me and plainly said, "Why wait?" He offered to baptize me that evening and said something else that stuck with me. "There are many things that could happen between now and next Sunday" He was referencing that none of us are promised tomorrow, so why wait? I said "OK, let's do it tonight."

I was back for evening service and at the end of it, the pastor called for the alter call. People that wanted to come down to the front and pray could come. I went towards the front to be taken upstairs for my baptism. The church had a large baptism pool in the upper loft. There was a stained glass window on the back wall that was just beautiful. They would have women and men line up separately if needed as the pool had two sides to enter into.

I went into a changing booth to take all of my clothes off and put on a church baptism robe; it was similar to a plain choir robe. Then I entered the baptism pool, while my minister friend was already in. He spoke to me about what I was getting ready to do and if I understood what I was doing. He then read Acts 2:38-39 to me and put his Bible down on the ledge. He put me under the water and when I came up, I had stammering lips. I had just taken a life-changing step into a full relationship with the Lord Jesus Christ.

You see, I was trying to go deeper the last few weeks and had the beginning stages of stammering lips before being baptized. I would call that the infant stage of speaking in the heavenly language or speaking in tongues. I had heard people in church speak eloquently in tongues but they had the gift of the Holy Spirit for quite some time or for many years.

When I went back to the changing room I could not stop physically shaking, it was more like a shiver. It was not because of being cold, the church kept the water pleasantly warm. I also had stammering lips that seemed like they did not want to stop. I had just received the gift of the Holy Spirit and this was a brand new me! Praise God!

I had heard that preached for weeks and now I had experienced it for myself. My Holy Ghost birthday as my friends would call it was and is August 4th. Exactly one month after arriving in Colorado, God had blessed me with the most personal intimate gift.

The greatest gift was Jesus dying on the cross for my sins so that I would not have to. I had entered into a relationship with Him, by repenting of my sins, asking for forgiveness of my sins, and asking Him to come into my heart to be with me. Believing that He did die on the cross and was resurrected from the dead on the third day and ascended into Heaven shortly thereafter. The Bible says:

> *That if thou shalt confess with thy mouth the Lord Jesus, and shalt believe in thine heart that God hath raised him from the dead, thou shalt will be saved.*
>
> Romans 10:9

Eternal life is something most people do not think of that often. Many people are walking around that mistakenly believe that this is it. When you die, you are buried and that's it, it's all over. These are the same people that have some of the attitudes like; get all that you can get in this life because that's all there is. Some joke about selling their souls to the devil while others claim to believe that there is no God. How can people be so deceived?

The evidence of God is all around us. We see it in nature, with the seasons and how the plants and trees come back year after year going through each season of spring, summer, fall, and winter. Look up at the night sky and see the handiwork of God.

The heavens declare the glory of God

Psalms 19:1

There are many verses that I could continue to share, but you, my friend have to reach the end of yourself and come back to God. He never left, you did. If you look deep in your heart, you know that the cares of this world pulled you away and you left voluntarily. Come back to God, He is waiting for you.

Chapter 66 Takeaway: Being Renewed

I had come a long way to be where I was but I had to be open to Biblical truth.
God had been preparing me for that very special day.
Are you ready to go deeper with God?

Bible verses to reflect upon:
Deuteronomy 6:5
Acts 2:38-39

Chapter 67

The Holy Spirit

Shortly after receiving the gift of the Holy Spirit, things started to happen to me. You know how we all have a conscience, that inner guide to our being that tells us the difference between right things and wrong things.

What was spoken in the baptism pool over me was the following Bible verses from King James Version (KJV) Acts 2:38-39

> *"Then Peter said unto them, Repent, and be baptized every one of you in the name of Jesus Christ for the remission of sins, and ye shall receive the gift of the Holy Ghost. For the promise is unto you, and to your children, and to all that are afar off, even as many as the Lord our God shall call"*

The Pentecostal church still uses the term Holy Ghost much more than Holy Spirit and teaches predominately from the KJV. The King James Bible was translated from 1604 until 1611 when it was then published. It is the most thoroughly accurate version of the Bible that we have today. They spent seven years translating the scriptures from the original Hebrew and Greek.

The next Sunday morning, I was in church and I had a conviction about going home and going through my music collection. It was a conviction as in you should go home and look at your music collection. It was not condemnation or down-putting in tone in any way. When I arrived home, I went to my large media cabinet that had decades of music compact discs, and DVDs of television and movies. I began looking at all of the music that I had. My collection was organized alphabetically and then chronologically. I had hundreds of CDs by dozens of artists. I began in the "A's" and as I started, I looked at the back of each CD, as that is where almost every one of those artists listed their song tracks. I first looked for anything that glorified hell or the devil then proceeded to look for anything hateful or anger-driven. I had spent the last quarter-century listening to various levels of heavy metal and hard rock music. Heavy metal is an angry genre and most of my music collection fell into that category.

I had picked up the kitchen trashcan and was going to be throwing away all of that music. It did not take me long to hear my old flesh rise up. I believe I was only into the "D's" when I had the thought, that I was throwing thousands of dollars worth of music away. As soon as I finished that thought I heard in the spirit "You can't put a price on your soul." That was the Holy Spirit encouraging me to keep going.

As I went through that process, I also had to look at artists that I had from the 1960s from the psychedelic era of rock-n-roll. They all went in the trash too because they all had written songs about drug use and free sex. They were glorifying sex out of marriage and the promotion of illegal and dangerous drug usage.

I filled two trash bags with hundreds of CDs from dozens of artists. At that time in Denver, we had small dumpsters in the alley that were generally shared by a couple of neighbors. I took all of the CDs out to the dumpster and prayed that no one would find them. When I went back into the house, I immediately thought of the stacks of heavy metal magazines and guitar player magazines that I had in old crates.

I brought out a crate of magazines that were full of photos and articles about bands. Some of those dated back to the late 1980s and early 1990s. I had bought those magazines new long ago. I set the whole crate of them on my coffee table and had to step out of the room for a moment. When I came back in, my one dog was gone, sitting in the spare bedroom. Something had bothered him and I was about to find out what.

As I sat on the couch and just started to thumb through those old magazines looking for any bookmarks or personal notes, I saw it. Throughout the magazines, there were advertisements for albums, t-shirts, adult sex apparel, and marijuana smoking products. The most shocking part of what I saw was all of the satanic symbols and glorification of the devil in album advertisements. I felt in the spirit there was a presence of evil that rested in or on those old magazines.

The next crate had various guitar player magazines that came with sheet music for learning the songs by the artists I had just thrown away. All of those magazines went into the trash as well. I had finished with the house cleaning of my music collection and went outside to leave for the Sunday evening service. I decided to look in the dumpster and smiled at what I saw. My neighbor had done yard work and there was a big pile of leaves and branches covering the bags of music and magazines that I had thrown away. I had prayed no one would take them out of the trash and God answered!

Chapter 67 Takeaway: The Comforter

I had received the gift of the Holy Spirit with my baptism. He was guiding me by clearing things out of my home that went against God.
Have you received the gift of the Holy Spirit?

Bible verses to reflect upon:
Nehemiah 9:20
John 14:16

Chapter 68

Healing

Many things had happened in a short time. Looking back at Abraham in Genesis, I am reminded of this passage with what I am about to tell you:

Is any thing too hard for the Lord?

Genesis 18:14

There had been a series of health issues that happened in late 1995 leading up to a particular doctor visit. I had back-to-back kidney stone attacks and then persistent heartburn and went to see the family doctor. It was January 1996 and after being referred to a specialist, I had been scheduled to undergo some testing. It was not that long of an appointment and I was given the unpleasant news.

The doctor said I had Esophageal Reflux. I had no idea what that meant and he had to explain it to me. If you do not know, the esophagus has a sphincter valve at the bottom of it where the esophagus meets the stomach. This valve when it functions properly opens and closes every time you swallow liquid or food. Mine was stuck in the open position.

If that was not bad enough news, he gave me the two options that were available back then, pills or major surgery. I asked about the surgery and he explained that it was major surgery because they would be cutting me open to reach this valve that was almost in the center of my body. He further explained that they only had about a fifty percent success rate with the surgery. It only took him explaining that to me and I opted for the pills.

Now, I told you all of that to tell you about my healing miracle. Miracles are for today, my friends! Getting back to August 2013 and my church. I had been baptized in Jesus's name, received the gift of the Holy Spirit, and had thrown out all of my hard rock and heavy metal music.

One service shortly after all of that, I was down in the altar area praying. A young man, whom I did not know came up behind me and started praying in tongues. He had his hand on my back and then all of a sudden he reached around with his right hand and slipped it through between my chest and my right arm. He was praying in tongues and touching the center of my chest. At that moment, I was merely agreeing with him in prayer, as I was new to speaking in tongues. I said Hallelujah a couple of times and there was a shift that happened.

I felt what I would describe as liquid love coming out of his hand and penetrating my chest. There was a warm liquid feeling flowing through the center of my body. He then began to speak in English and prophecy over me. Making references to personal things that only God and I knew. Those things were about my journey and what God was calling me to. The young man did not know me nor did I know him.

The Lord was working through him to heal my body and to speak positive and good things over me at that moment. He was a willing vessel, he was surrendered to God and God used him to heal me. It was not him but it was God. When he finished praying over me, I felt better instantly. I felt amazing!

I caught up with the pastor in the lobby and shared the experience that I had just had and wanted to know what he thought. I had only been in the church a little over a month at that time. He got back to me not long after that and explained "the willing vessel" portion of what happened to me and for others if they will receive it. I had been on over-the-counter and prescription medicines for eighteen and a half years. In one moment, in a single service, God had healed me!

Chapter 68 Takeaway: Healing Hands

I had followed God and was seeking Him with my whole heart.
In an instant, He healed and restored my body.
Has God ever healed you?

Bible verses to reflect upon:
Isaiah 9:4
Romans 8:2

_____
_____
_____
_____
_____
_____
_____
_____
_____
_____
_____
_____

Chapter 69

Speak Lord

One early fall day, I had decided that I was going to go to a job fair. I had not had any success with obtaining employment up to that point.

The job fair was not even related to my industry but since I had management experience I thought it would carry over. I got dressed and had my resume ready to hand out to prospective employers. The job fair was about thirty minutes away and as I left my carport and got out onto the street, the Lord spoke. He said, "don't go to the job fair." I asked and thought in the spirit, where do you want me to go? The answer was the prayer room at the church. That room was on the ground floor with a separate entrance that had a keypad lock. You had to ask for and be given the access code and I had done so previously.

As I was praying and making the drive towards the church, I had this uncertain feeling about things. What was going on? I was closely watching my money dwindle each week, as I had no job or source of income. I thought I was doing the right thing that morning by preparing to go to that job fair.

The church was just over seven miles from my house and as I crossed through a major intersection about a mile or so from the church something happened. As soon as I was through it, the Lord came into my vehicle. I mean, He came in and was sitting in the passenger seat. I did not see the Lord but felt His presence, as it was the exact same feeling and massive shift in the atmosphere that happened less than one year ago on the top of that mountain.

Here He was with me in my vehicle. I was so overcome; I did not even know what to do, except to keep driving as I was on a busy road with traffic. The Lord spoke as tears were streaming down my face by just being in His presence. He spoke to me a clear message, a command to preach to the youth. Again, I could hardly speak because I was completely overwhelmed by His presence but I was able to ask a one-word question, how? He answered me and then left just as quickly as He had entered my vehicle. The wonderful, awesome presence of the Lord Jesus Christ lifted.

I was in another world after the experience and continued to drive to the church. Although, it felt like I was on autopilot for that last mile. I went into the prayer room and prayed about many things during the visit. I prayed a long while and then I did something that can only be explained as my own fleshly desire. I drove to the original location that I was headed to that morning. Once I got to the job fair, there were no jobs that I qualified for and really no jobs that I could see myself even doing. Why had I gone there?

The Lord had instructed me not to go to the job fair and had instead directed me to the church prayer room. On the way to the prayer room, He came into my vehicle and spoke to me. That was in the spirit but it was just like having an audible conversation with another person.

I mentioned being driven by the flesh. You would have thought I was on cloud nine after the Lord showed up and spoke to me. I was for quite a while but on the same day, just a few hours later here I was at the job fair. What happened? I was looking at dollars and was focused on earning a living to pay the bills. I had trusted God this far but was not trusting Him with money. Think about what I have shared with you up until this point. I did not know what had happened that day with the job fair and why but I was about to go into a season of learning how the kingdom works and learning to trust God more.

Chapter 69 Takeaway: Eyes Upon God

On an ordinary day, the miraculous happened. The Lord came and spoke with me.
He gave me instructions for the moment and what I was called to do.
Have you ever been so moved by God but later stumbled in your flesh?

Bible verses to reflect upon:
Proverbs 16:3
Romans 8:5-6

Chapter 70

Kingdom Driven

Jesus is talking about money and true riches in Luke 16:11-13:

> *If therefore ye have not been faithful in the unrighteous mammon, who will commit to your trust the true riches? And if ye have not been faithful in that which is another man's, who shall give you that which is your own? No servant can serve two masters: for either he will hate the one, and love the other; or else he will hold to the one, and despise the other. Ye cannot serve God and mammon.*

First of all what or who is mammon? Mammon is a very old spirit that rests on money. It is an Aramaic word that means riches but it comes from the Syrian god of riches. Its origins are from Babylon and the tower of Babel found in Genesis 11. Babel is defined as a confused noise made by a number of voices. The story of the tower reveals that the people of Babylon thought they could get to Heaven on their own and that they did not need God.

The spirit of mammon will say that we don't need God if we have riches and money. It is a contrasting spirit with the Spirit of God. The spirit will talk to you, especially if you are newly saved and in church. Give an offering and it will say that you can't give that much. It may say that you need all of your money, don't give it away! How then do we overcome and break the spirit of mammon?

Jesus talked about mammon in four passages of scripture. Luke 16: 9, 11, 13, and Matthew 6:24 which is from the account we find in the book of Luke. It is interesting that Luke is the only one that records this and it is with great detail. That is why we have the four gospels. Looking at Luke 16:9-10 we see the following:

> *9. And I say unto you, Make to yourselves friends of the mammon of unrighteousness; that, when ye fail, they may receive you into everlasting habitations. 10. He that is faithful in that which is least is faithful also in much: and he that is unjust in the least is unjust also in much.*

What Jesus is talking about in verse nine is using your money for the things of God. By giving a tithe you not only break off the spirit of mammon but you also bless the kingdom of God. You make friends through church, the church shares the gospel through many outlets and your friends will become saved.

When you fail, here it means to die; they will receive you into everlasting habitations, which are dwellings. The reference to everlasting habitations is Heaven and being received by your friends that heard the gospel because you gave to the kingdom of God. In verse ten Jesus is talking about being faithful in that which is least, money.

In verse eleven as He continues, He is talking about not being faithful in the unrighteous mammon, how then can you be trusted with true riches? What are true riches? He is talking about people He is talking about souls. In verse twelve He is talking about tithes. Let us now look at Malachi 3:10-11

> *Bring ye all the tithes into the storehouse, that there may be meat in mine house, and prove me now herewith, saith the LORD of hosts, If I will not open you the windows of heaven, and pour you out a blessing, that there shall not be room enough to receive it. And I will rebuke the devourer for your sakes, and he shall not destroy the fruits of your ground; neither shall your vine cast her fruit before the time in the field, saith the LORD of hosts.*

And in Luke 16:13 He says No servant can serve two masters. Ye cannot serve God and mammon. To break the spirit of mammon, all money needs to be redeemed. You do this each time you are paid by returning ten percent, the tithe, to God and He blesses the ninety percent that remains. To finish that statement, let us look at Malachi 3:8-11:

> *Will a man rob God? Yet ye have robbed me. But ye say, Wherein have we robbed thee? In tithes and offerings. Ye are cursed with a curse: for ye have robbed me, even this whole nation. Bring ye all the tithes into the storehouse, That there may be meat in mine house, and prove me now herewith, saith the LORD of hosts, if I will not open you the windows of heaven, and pour out a blessing, that there shall not be room enough to receive it. And I will rebuke the devourer for your sakes, and he shall not destroy the fruits of your ground; neither shall your vine cast her fruit before the time in the field, saith the LORD of hosts.*

The last scripture I want to share about finances is from 1Timothy 6:10:

> *For the love of money is the root of all evil: which while some coveted after, they have erred from the faith, and pierced themselves through with many sorrows.*

This is one of the most misquoted scriptures of all time. Money is not the root of all evil; it is the love of money. It is how you choose to use it, my friend. God is the only one who can turn money into souls. Be a good steward of what God has blessed you with.

This was a hard lesson for me to learn. During my period of not having new money coming in, I was afraid to give and did so sparingly. When the job came and I began to work, I then looked at bills first and tithing last. I even tithed on the "net" for some time. It finally came together for me through the teaching I was under from a television preacher in Dallas, Texas. He taught many series of messages in his style of teaching preaching. It was only then that I began to tithe on the "gross." That means that you put God first. Putting God above all taxes, insurance, and retirement.

A tithe is ten percent, simply stated if you make $100 you tithe $10. You bring the tithe back to God; you return it to His storehouse. Preferably to your local church where you are spiritually fed, have a pastor, and where you can receive prayer. An offering is just that. It is between you and God and it is a private matter just as tithing is. Offerings can go to your local church, other churches like I have mentioned on television or radio, and local charities. That is between you and God.

Chapter 70 Takeaway: Tithes and Offerings

Learning how to trust God with all of my finances took longer than it should have for me. I finally got the revelation of tithing to God and what an offering truly is.
Are you a faithful and cheerful giver to God?

Bible verses to reflect upon:
Proverbs 3:9-10
2 Corinthians 9:7

In Closing

I pray that my story has edified you, encouraged you and helped you on your journey to a life full of spiritual riches as you walk with the Lord Jesus Christ.

Thank you so much for your support as God continues to guide me in sharing the good news of the gospel and overcoming addictions and having victory in this life

Contact Information

Shane Tempel Ministries LC
PO Box 51687
Casper, WY 82605

307-298-9440

Email: info@shanetempelministries.com

www.shanetempelministries.com

www.ingramcontent.com/pod-product-compliance
Lightning Source LLC
Chambersburg PA
CBHW050336010526
44119CB00037B/466/J